Born Again Texan!

A Newcomer's Guide To Texas

Robin Cole

Republic of Texas Press
Plano, Texas

Library of Congress Cataloging-in-Publication Data

Cole, Robin, 1942-.
  Born again Texan : a newcomer's guide to Texas / Robin Cole.
    p. cm.
  Includes bibliographical references.
  ISBN 1-55622-730-2
  1. Texas—Description and travel. 2. Texas—Social life and customs
  3. Texas—Guidebooks. I. Title.
  F391.2.C65 1999
  917.6404'63—dc21   99-048505
                                     CIP

Republic of Texas Press is an imprint of Wordware Publishing, Inc.
No part of this book may be reproduced in any form or by
any means without permission in writing from
Wordware Publishing, Inc.

Printed in the United States of America

ISBN 1-55622-730-2
10 9 8 7 6 5 4 3 2
9910

All inquiries for volume purchases of this book should be addressed to
Wordware Publishing, Inc., at 2320 Los Rios Boulevard, Plano, Texas
75074. Telephone inquiries may be made by calling:

(972) 423-0090

Dedications

To Dixie who called me back to Texas

To Richard who actually fetched me

To Vic who gave me a reason to stay

To Alisa who always believed in me

To Jesse and Jade who showed me the way

To Ginnie Bivona who gave me a chance

To Karen Wright who believed I could write even before I did write

To Victoria, Robert, Donna, Belle, Micky, Kari, Sandy, Robin, Caren and Bob, Lisa, Kaycee, Ann and John, Tedra and Neal for your support and inspiration

To Cathy who gave me my title

And to Jon McConal who had the good sense to never leave Texas for too long

Contents

Introduction

The sun shot through the threatening storm clouds, making golden the highway ahead of me. I crossed the state line—it was a mystical experience—my hair got big, I got my accent back, I laughed out loud, and I was BORN AGAIN TEXAN!

I was the prodigal daughter, Houston bred, returning to my native state after a mere thirty-year absence. I had escaped, I arrogantly thought, right after college and headed for the "real world." I wanted to see it all. If I had been rich, I would have traveled, but since I was poor, I just moved and moved and moved some more.

I tried to live in states with no distinguishing geographic shape. You know, those squares stacked in the middle of the weather map with just two seasons—winter and the 4th of July.

I checked out the right coast and the left coast and overheard pompous, uninformed comments about the Lone Star State. I lost my accent and lived in glitter cities where it's hard to tell the real folks from the plastic prop extras. I had my share of tofu, raw fish, imported water, and toothpick sized vegetables.

I got used to being served in stores by kids with spiky, eggplant-colored hair who talked on the phone, chewed gum, and couldn't have recognized me in a lineup if I had shot them—which I was tempted to do.

Through a series of cosmic events, failed marriages, and corporate downsizings, I joined thousands of others from all over the country and the world who move to Texas each year. If you are one of those pilgrims, let me assure you, I had forgotten more than you never knew about this great state.

For example, here in Texas, religion is political, politics is sport, and sport is religion. We are not southern, that's Mississippi, or southwestern, that's Arizona. And certainly we are not western, that's Montana and Wyoming, who are just wannabees. No, we are Texans and damn proud of it.

May I welcome y'all to Texas with the assurance that no matter where you hail from (we know you got here just as soon as you could), transformation can be yours. I even know some folks from New Jersey who have been saved. There are new rules to play by, codes and secret vows to be discovered, and a new language to be learned. Study real hard, and God willin' and the creeks don't rise y'all can be BORN AGAIN TEXAN!

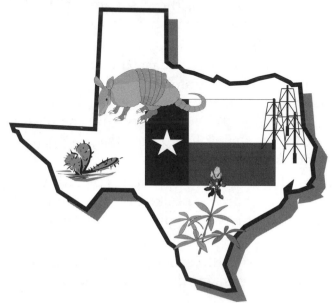

Foreword

By Jon McConal

I make my living interviewing Texans and writing about them. Without exception the people whom I meet and talk with are all characters, particularly the ones who have been born and reared in this state.

I seldom do my interviews by telephone. I like looking a person in the eye. You will discover something about this person that will never be captured from a telephone interview. Maybe it's the smell of bacon frying in the background or the way a person looks you in the eye—most Texans look you in the eye. Regardless, a personal interview adds strength and truth to a writer's story.

These points are why I like this delightful little book by Robin Cole. Time and again, she captures this thing that so many people enjoy about Texans. I think this comes from her deep sensitivity about the state and the fact that she has been to the places she describes. Thank gosh she has come home.

I like the way she describes the real people. Her stories paint accurate pictures of the kind of people I have met and talked with during my forty years as a writer. I particularly liked the stories told by her great-grandmother. She is my kind of Texan.

Cole's writing about the way Texans talk is hilarious. Her samples bring laughter even from us natives. One example is a Texan asking a friend for a favor.

"Would you carry me to the hardware store?"

"You betja," came the reply.

Her keen observations of Texans may sound like exaggerations to those who are not natives. But to those reared here, we know that things found in the back of a pickup truck do indeed include various rusted machine parts that are totally unrelated and a security alarm system that is a dawg named Killer.

She touches on all the things that so many find strange in our state: from our cuisine—that includes such items as the kitchen sink tomato sandwich, a concoction made from tomatoes brought in straight from the garden, sliced, and layered on two slices of white bread choked with mayonnaise; and our famed chicken-fried steak—to our driving habits and our fascination with the weather. And Cole gives us an interesting and easy read of the history of our state.

The book is not only for newcomers. Natives will find many new attractions, from nightclubs to restaurants to recipes, in here. And, there are the characters like the woman who dances mostly alone at a nightclub—a touching love story.

I have never met this writer, but I am glad she came to her senses and moved back to Texas. I will be damned glad to shake her hand and maybe even open the door of her pickup for her some day. That's one of the things that Cole says us natives still do and the women still appreciate.

Jon McConal's heartwarming columns about Texans appear three days a week in the Fort Worth Star-Telegram.

A Born Again/Newbee Texan's Ten Commandments

☆

1) Never forget: religion is political, politics is sport, and sport is religion.

2) The titles of "ma'am" and "sir" are offered as a sign of respect, not a comment on your age.

3) A real male Texan WILL open the door, pull out a chair, walk on the outside, and pay the check for a lady.

4) A real female Texan knows how to change a tire but lets a man do it anyway.

5) Don't ever brag about how things are done where you came from, 'cause we don't care.

6) When a Texan says, "Well, now, to tell yew the truth, now that I thank about it..." history is about to be rewritten.

7) How people are dressed or what they are drivin' will give you no clue as to their net worth.

8) Never bite the tip off a chili pepper, especially if the one handing it to you says, "Try it! They's reeeeal mild."

9) After you've lived in a small Texas town for twenty-seven years, you'll still be a "newcomer."

10) There's nothing small about small talk in Texas. You'll be judged by it. So, study up!!

Texas Weather Watch

I vividly remember the moment I decided to come home to Texas. I was staring up at the undercarriage of my car. Having slipped on the ice while pouring kitty litter under the wheels, I was trying to get some traction in order to back out over a berm of snow that was as tall as I am—so I could get out of my garage. I was in Lake Tahoe. It is a glorious place to visit, but I was living there. I decided to move to a better climate.

I had obviously forgotten, we don't have a climate in Texas—we just have weather. We figure God was just showin' off and decided to put everything in one state. We have just about any kind of weather you've ever heard of, and it comes on so fast you won't know what hit you. We watch the TV weather report for sheer entertainment, especially if some idiot is actually making PREDICTIONS. It's even more fun if the prognosticator is brand new and from out of state. The old-timers know it's gonna be hot, cold, wet, dry, or windy and maybe all before noon.

In the hot category, you have your dry heat and your humid heat—and it's all hot. It can be hot in January, and it's always hot in August. "Hot enough for you?" is a civil salutation most of the year round. Back in 1980 temperatures shot up to the triple digits and stayed there for the month of July. This is why we all own property in Colorado. Texans didn't do much movin' around until air conditioning came along. Now we live, drive, work, shop, worship, and dine in cold air most of the year. Ladies always carry a "wrap" with them in order to fend off the teeth chattering chill of refrigerated interiors. You can always spot the tourists in restaurants because they are shivering in their tank tops.

Cold to a Texan is anytime the thermometer dips below 70 degrees. We dig out our coats, sweaters, and scarves and whine, "Aren't you cold? I'm so cold!" This salutation is good about three times a year, as is all outerwear. That is unless you are in the Panhandle, where "blue northers" can drop temperatures eighty degrees in an hour, and winds blow sleet and baseball-sized hail horizontally over the frozen terrain. They say if you see more than thirteen blackbirds sitting on a fence, you had better get ready for a norther. In 1899 one attacked the whole state, and Dallas firemen had to start a fire to thaw out a water hydrant. Cattle froze in South Texas and the skies dumped half a foot of snow. That storm froze up Galveston Bay, and the temperature in Tulia dropped to –23 degrees. There's a tale of a cowpoke who got knocked out, froze, and blown down to Mexico. He thawed out, woke up, and now lives on tequila shots bought by folks who just want to hear his story.

Then you got your hailstorms and ice storms. Ice storms literally freeze up towns—schools close, and nobody goes nowhere, 'cause nobody knows how to drive on ice. These ice storms happen on one of those three cold days in winter. Your hailstorms happen anytime they please but mostly in hot months like the one that dropped softball-sized hail on Hockley County for the better part of an hour on an August day in 1979. It beat the heck out of crops to the tune of two hundred million dollars.

Wet means torrential rains and hurricanes. Wet means floods as creeks become ragin' rivers, gullies wash out bridges, and livestock learn to swim. Wet means dark, loud, rollin' storms that thunder out of the Gulf of Mexico, horrifying, devastating windstorms that smash into the coast with cute names—like Camille, Audrey, or Tiffany. I think the names got cuter after hurricane Beulah spat out about 115 tornadoes in a five-day horror show back in 1967.

Dry is an outstanding category. You won't know a real drought until you are introduced to one in Texas. Sometimes out in West Texas it's dry for so long there are ducks that never learn to swim, and folks at the fillin' station have to pay more for water than for gas. The guys at the bars have to settle for no "water backs" with their drinks and watchin' girls "dust wrassel." Serious prayer is reserved for an extended drought; the longer it lasts, the larger the church attendance gets.

Wind is such a big part of Texas weather that when it isn't blowin' you kinda get scared. You get used to swoops and swallows of dust and pushing open the door with one hand while restyling your hair with the other on the way into the air-conditioned building. Sometimes winds get psychotic and whirl dervish-style in storm clouds, reaching long pointy fingers to earth, clearing paths with precise destruction. The state is in "Tornado Alley," and no other state has as many tornadoes in a year. There's nothin' quite like a Texas tornado.

I had some friends who left their place one calm sunny morning to go into town. Their house, chicken coop, and barn stood side by side. A tornado hit while they were gone, and they rushed back, afraid of what they might find. The house and barn stood unharmed in the hot sun, but the chicken coop was gone. It had been removed as if by a giant surgeon's knife. They found chickens plucked naked, sunburned, and wandering drunkenly through the fields. They claimed that all they could lay from then on was scrambled eggs.

Learnin' Texanese

As a college freshman (don't ask when, I don't remember) I had an insurmountable language barrier with my roommate. No, neither of us was an exchange student. I was from Texas, and she was from Texas. We were attending a Texas college, but we couldn't communicate:

"Ore yew frum baack East?" she asked.

"I'm from Houston," I responded, hoping I had guessed right about the question.

"Ohhhh, wayll yew kinda saound like a yaankee." We were off to a great start.

One day she asked if I had "a pace a strang," which I finally deciphered meant a piece of string. I said, "Oh, string rhymes with ring."

"Thaat's whut I said—strang like rang."

Of course I had an accent, too. She got her licks in about the dumb way I said, "tea."

"Yew saay 'tee' like 'tee-tee,'" she would laugh. She pronounced it "taay."

When you figure the state is almost eight hundred miles from Texarkana to El Paso, there's bound to be some regional differences, but some expressions work just about anywhere. Here are a few phrases to help you communicate with the natives.

Texas Phrase	Translation
Y'all	You guys—always plural
All y'all	All you guys

Fixin'	Getting ready to or preparing
Holler at me	Give me a call

"I just thought I'd holler at y'all 'cause I'm fixin' enough dinner to feed Cox's army, and I want all y'all to come." You had better check to see if they mean at noon or at 6:00, for at some places dinner is at noon and supper is the evening meal.

Discount what you see in the movies. Texans don't refer to a single individual as y'all. When I left the state I replaced y'all with "you guys." I felt like Carlo Leone and had a strong desire for Haitian cigars when I used the term, but it was the only substitute I could find for this warm, inclusive, endearing term.

Texans are always fixin' to do something. My mother told me the other day that an imported friend of hers had asked, "Dixie, why are you people always 'fixing' dinner, is it broken?" Mom answered, "Well, I'm not really sure but with all the fixin' tos and fixin' ofs you'd think we'd be in good repair!"

Howdy	Hi
Hot enough for you	Hi
Oooo, I'm cold, are you cold?	Hi
Zaat you?	Hi
Well, I'll be!	Hi
Wind blow you in?	Hi
Wal I'll be dern	Hi

Greetings are an important part of any venture into town as everyone greets you. A clever salutation is an important part of how your character is judged. You need to "ask after" the spouse and kids, mention the weather, and complain about the gov'ment, but most importantly coax a chuckle or, better yet, a belly laugh. Everyone in Texas is a comedian. "Zaat you, Earl, you ole sidewinder, wind blow you into town? Whars that pretty woman puts up with you? By the size of your gut I sure can tell she cooks as good as she looks."

Mess	Upset, disheveled	She was a mess.
Mess	Large amount	I'm makin' a mess of beans.
Mess	Cute	Jr's a little mess.
Mess	Litter	Don't mess with Texas.
Messin'	Making out	They were just messin' around.
Messin'	Teasing	Are you messin' with me?
Bawl	Cry	They were bawlin' like babies.
Ball	Good time	We had a ball.

In some parts of the state ladies might be startled when a gent asks, "So, you wanna go ballin'?" He is probably just inviting you to go bowling. Ball can also mean boil, as in "ballin' mad."

Tump (mostly with over)	Tip and dump	Oh, he tumped over his tea!

I went out into the rest of the world thinking "tump" was an American word. I was stunned when folks laughed at me when I used it. It is a perfectly good, highly descriptive word. Anything can be tumped—from eighteen wheelers, "There it was, just tumped over on the bridge," to people, "He ain't so tough—a two-year-ol' could tump him over."

'Spose	Suppose	I 'spose so.
Chunk	Throw	Were you boys chunkin' rocks?
Spoilt	Gone bad,	Taste this and see if it's spoilt.
	Bratty	His mommy has spoilt him.
Het up	Mad, hot	
Pissed off	Mad	

Texans have many clever ways to let you know that someone is angry. You don't want to be around if, "she's havin' a hissy fit" or "he's blowin' a gasket," because they might "raise a ruckus" and "let you have it with both barrels."

Although some may think of Texans as being braggarts, we really don't care much for folks who "put on airs," "get biggity," "uppity," "get on their high horse," or act like they're in "high cotton," meaning rich. The ever-eloquent Temple Houston, Sam's lawyer son, once commented that a colleague was so arrogant, "He can strut sitting down." So be careful not to "blow smoke" or folks might think you are "all flash and no substance."

Texans want to make themselves perfectly clear. In order to accomplish this, many important statements begin with, "Now, I'm gonna tell you the truth, and I mean it," and finish with "and you can take that to the bank!"

Reach me that	Hand me that	Reach me the catsup, please.
Diddly squat	Worthless	He ain't worth diddly squat.
Thing-a-majig	A thang	Almost anything
Whatsamacallit	A thang	Almost anything

Carry	Take	Could you carry me to town?
You betja	Correct, yes	"That right?" "You betja."
Much obliged	Thanks a lot	

"Could you carry me to the hardware store?"

"You betja."

"Well, I'm much obliged, I gotta get a new thing-a-majig for my whatsamacallit, 'cause mine ain't worth diddly squat."

Mighty	Very	That's a mighty purty dress, Ma'am.
Right	Very	That's a right purty dress, Ma'am.
Plum	Very	That's a plum purty dress, Ma'am.

The Lone Star State can make allowances for eccentric behavior and be forgiving of mistakes, but we cannot abide stupidity. If you've got no horse sense, don't know diddly squat, haven't got the sense God gave a stump, have a single digit IQ, are not the sharpest knife in the drawer, or are one brick shy of a load, then you are dumb as a box of rocks, and we will mess with you. As the ol' sayin' goes, I can explain it to ya, but I can't understand it for ya.

Umpteen	A lot
Heap	Umpteen
Passel	A heap
Mess	Passel

I've told you umpteen times that you'll be in a heap of trouble with your Ma iffin you don't eat that mess of grits.

Thoughty	Kind, considerate	That was mighty thoughty of y'all.
Cattywampus	Mixed up, confused	You got that all cattywampus, boy.
	Out of alignment	How cum your bumper's all cattywampus?
Stewed	Drunk	
Drowned	Drunker	
Knee-walkin'	Drunk some more	
Pie-eyed	Drunkest	

When Jake gets pie-eyed, a passel of thangs get all cattywampus. He tumped over his truck last time he got stewed and plum near ruined his thing-a-majig. He got himself in a mess of trouble with the law, but didn't diddly squat happen since he is the mayor.

Texas Names

≥ ★ ≤

When my granddaughter, Jade, was born, my grandson was just three and thrilled about his new sister. Jesse crawled into my lap the evening of that special day and stared up at me, patting my cheek. "Grandma Robin aren't you just so happy we had a little baby girl?" he asked. I told him I certainly was so happy. He patted my face thoughtfully and then he said, "And aren't you so happy that we named her middle name after you?" I assured him I was so happy about that. He patted my face and said slowly, "Jade . . . Grandma Robin . . . is her name!"

Texans are proud of Texas and other Texans. We named our towns and cities after people, and we name our people after towns and cities. You will meet a lot of kids named Austin, Dallas, Worth, Tyler, Houston, Burnet, Temple, Laredo, Odessa, Antonio, Jefferson, Cooper, Angelo, Cleburne, Victoria, Clifton, and Wallis and Willis. Our map also features towns with normal people names like Alice, Benjamin, Henrietta, Irene, Josephine, Justin, Kenney, Lillian, Lorenzo, Marietta, Troy, Vera, Vick, and Wallis and Willis.

Mostly we know who towns are named after like Austin (the Father of Texas) and Houston (for Sam), but Dallas isn't too sure which Dallas it's named for. You don't find a lot of little Chicagos, Bostons, and Sacramentos running around, do you? Wyoming has its share of Codys, Jacksons, and Cheyennes, but they also have a lot of Austins and Dallases, because Wyoming was settled by Texans. Oh, they might try to tell you different, but how else can you explain the similarities in our cultures?

Colorado may have a Denver or two, but they mostly name their kids Tiffany and Chance.

You have probably heard a great deal about how we like to have two front names and use them both, and that is somewhat true. You've got your Jim Bobs, Jimmy Joes, Joe Bobs, and Bobby Jims. You've also got your Kelli Sues, Christi Lous, your Tori Lees, Suzi Bees, and your Tammi Lynns and Brandi Gins, and there has been a long-standing rule that for girls at least one of the two front names must end in "i."

My grandfather had six front names, so his brothers always teased him that he must be triplets.

We are big into unisex names but try to distinguish the boys from the girls with the ending "i" or "y." The boys get that "y" gene you know. So you have your Traci and Tracey, Casie and Casey, and Jerri and Jerry. But "ie"s can be either. You following me so far? Texas men love to have children named after them—boys or girls. The feminizing of traditional men's names means you'll be meeting Claudene, Bobbette, Earlene, Willamena, Alane, Elmera, Norvella, Thedisa, and Ozella (named for her daddy, Ozelle).

Since so many of our family names go way back and are honored by each generation, we wind up with many folks all named the same names in one family. That's where tacking on Junior, Big, Little, and Tiny comes in handy.

It really doesn't matter how many names you have because if people like you, they are gonna give you a nickname. If they don't like you, they are gonna give you a nickname for sure, you just won't hear it to your face.

You will soon discover that a trip around the world can be yours within the Texas borders. You can travel to Athens, Dublin, Egypt, Holland, Iraan, Ireland, Italy, London, Naples, Paris, Scotland, Turkey, and China. Or perhaps you would prefer to "see America" with stops in Cleveland, Frisco, Georgetown, Lincoln, Memphis, Nevada, Omaha, Universal City, Washington, and West Point.

Or if you are feeling a little frisky, you may want to be reminded of the old saying, "Texas girls bathe in Sweetwater and dress in Plainview. The boys go to Seymour."

As I have warned you, Texans like to mess with you. There are towns with booby trap names that you won't have a clue how to pronounce. This was done on purpose so we know you aren't from around "these parts," and we can sell you jackalope bait. I'll try to help you out here, but just remember to step lightly when trying to say the name of a place here in Texas.

There is the story about the two traveling salesmen who drove into Mexia and began to argue about how the town's name was pronounced.

"I say it's Mex-ee-uh."

"Well, I know it's Muh-HAY-uh."

They decided in order to settle the argument once and for all, they would stop for coffee and ask a native. They ordered and when the waitress brought the coffee, one of the men asked, "Miss, could you please tell us how you pronounce the name of this place?" Slowly and distinctly, she said, "DAAIRRRRREEEEEE QUEEEEEN!"

Some folks have trouble with the likes of Luckenbach, (LOO-kin-bahk), Balmorhea (bal-moh-RAY), or Refugio (reh-FYOOR-ih-oh). Sometimes even the residents of a town can't agree on how to pronounce their town name. *The Dallas Morning News* reported that residents of Rowlett were divided as to whether it was ROW-let or row-LETT.

Don't think you know how to pronounce something because you are familiar with a foreign language. Sometimes we have just Texasized the word. Like Boerne is BER-nee, Llano is LAN-o, and the Bosque River is the BOSS-key.

The little town of Comfort was originally named Gemetlichkeit, a German word meaning tranquillity. Betcha Texans could have had a field day with that one. Reklaw was named in honor of Margaret Walker as the town was established on her land. The name Walker was already chosen by another community, thus Reklaw—Walker spelled backwards.

Colorado City isn't in Colorado County, but it is on the Colorado River. For a very long time the citizens of Colorado City pronounced their town's name Col-oo-ray-do, but nowadays most everyone agrees on saying it like the Rocky Mountain state.

You'll find West in the east and Eastland to the west of West, Westphalia, and Westover. Austonio is nowhere near either Austin or San Antonio. Got it? Study all of the above and then we'll move on to Falfurrias, Seguin, and Pflugerville.

Texas Critters

Unless you are migrating from the Galapagos Islands, you will be impressed by the variety of varmints and critters Texas has to offer. The ground literally undulates and vibrates beneath your feet with writhing, burrowing, earth moving creatures. Beware, most of them are capable of inflicting grave bodily harm.

Mosquitoes, spiders, chiggers, scorpions, and fire ants firmly believe that humans are beneath them on the food chain. They will lick the insect repellent off you and bite you. They will fly at you, jump on you, crawl up you, lower themselves from ceilings to reach you and bite you. They are larger than the pantywaist pests you have encountered in other places, and they are vicious.

Having grown up in Houston, I believed that all air was sauna-sweaty, all skies were gray, and all bugs were bigger than house pets. A Houston cockroach can move furniture. Mosquitoes stare you in the eye while they suck your blood. Tiny fire ants are new to me as they were imported while I was gone. I was introduced to the little devils my first Fourth of July back. I was foolishly standing in the grass wearing sandals while watching a parade. Texas grass is not intended to be walked on, just viewed, and sandals are to be worn only indoors. The fire ant attack was sudden and well organized. I felt as if hot acid had been splashed on my feet. I jumped so high I bounded onto the chamber of commerce float, did a wild, screaming interpretive dance, and received a round of applause. The little blisters and welts lasted weeks, and the fiery itching was relentless. There are all kinds of fire ant killers on the market. None of them work. The vociferous little devils just retrench with added fortitude to look for sandals and tenderfoots.

There are alligators in the wetlands and in the mountains—lions. I'm not kiddin', they call them mountain lions. Armadillos and horny toads are armored, Jurassic Park escapees. Why did the armadillo cross the road? Nobody knows as not one of them has ever made it. That's why they are called Texas speed bumps. Horny toads are ugly little lizards that kids bring home to keep as pets. They make them little harnesses so they can pull around match boxes. Kids torment them because if you scare one good, it will spit blood from its eyeballs. It doesn't take a lot to entertain our little Texans.

Snakes are everywhere. There are grass snakes in the grass, copperheads in the bushes, and guess where the water moccasins are? We have more lakes than Minnesota, "the land of 1,000 lakes," and there are snakes in just about all of them. Water-skiers have more to be concerned about than sunburn. You will need to learn the good snakes from the bad ones. Supposedly snakes with blunt tails are poisonous, and sharp pointed tailed snakes are nonpoisonous. Or just assume, as I do, that the only good snakes are the dead ones. But as the old saying goes, "A dead snake can still bite." Just assume this is true, and save yourself a trip to the emergency room.

Prairie dogs are very sophisticated rodents that build "towns"—no lie—like one discovered in 1905. It stretched for 250 miles and housed about 400 million prairie dogs, complete with little skyscrapers and little tiny taxis.

White-tail deer are graceful, elegant creatures that like to wait in the bushes at the side of winding hill country roads at dusk and then dive into the road in front of your car. I figure they are showing the armadillos where to park. If there is one deer, there are thirteen more coming. They are so used to people that they graze in your flower-beds, and when you aren't looking they'll crawl into your hot tub.

Way down on the southern tip of the state you've got your Texas tortoises that live on little islands known as lomas. They tend to be hermits, so each has its own island.

Each March, Braken Cave near San Antonio hosts the Mexican free-tailed bat convention. Usually about twenty million bats show up to party hearty, getting drunk and participating in hanky-panky that results in a summer baby bat boom. The Air Force wanted to close Braken Cave—with a bomb—because the bats were messin' up their radar. A group called Bat Conservation International stopped that plan. The BCI group is based in Austin, of course. Our state capital is real proud of its bat population. Folks toast them with champagne when the bats do their evening escape from under the bridge. Most of us have been worried about Austin folks for some time now. People in West Texas think it's probably because they are gettin' too much oxygen from all those trees that block their view.

We have got more wild cats than any other state—lots of bobcats and mountain lions, also referred to as pumas, cougars, panthers, and wildcats. Ocelots and jaguarundi are rarer and on the endangered species list. Texans call the jaguarundi "weasel-cats" because nobody can pronounce jaguarundi.

Raccoons are cute little guys with bandit masks and hands more delicate than a brain surgeon's. Curiosity is a raccoon's middle name. Never has a feed room been constructed that a raccoon can't penetrate. Before scolding your dog for making a shambles of the outdoor trash, be sure and check for raccoon handprints. The opposite of raccoon is opossum. Possums are ugly, ghostly blobs that hang from trees at night and scare your dog. They also are attracted to pet food left on the back porch. But don't be alarmed when you catch a glimpse of one up close, they aren't dead, just "possuming."

Texas squirrels assume the identity and character of their region. Town squirrels are jealous of their rural buddies and are suicidal, often frying themselves on power lines. Big city pet stores will sell you cayenne pepper-laced birdseed that they guarantee is squirrel proof. Don't believe it if you reside in far East Texas. The Cajun squirrels send up smoke signals to all their buddies to come celebrate Mardi Gras at the Jones's new bird feeder.

Coyotes (correctly pronounced with two syllables in Texas) are hated by ranchers, loved by environmentalists, and revered by cowboy poets. Cowboy poets are another critter category altogether. They wear their fancy boots on the outside of their pants, sport cute little neckerchiefs and oversized hats, and have names like "Badger" and "Mesquite."

Mesquite trees are not literally varmints, but the way ranchers and farmers have to fight them, they might as well be. You clear a pasture in the morning, and they are back after lunch. Some say at the end of time, the last things remaining in Texas will be a coyote standing in a fire ant bed underneath a mesquite tree. Oh well, at least the environmentalists will be happy.

Vehicles and Such

⇟ ⭐ ⇞

Texans love their vehicles. Cars, trucks, vans, or tractors, they're all vehicles. "Zat your vehicle? How's it workin' fer ya?" I guess this is because we take the Department of Motor Vehicles a little more seriously than they do elsewhere. We like 'em big as all outdoors, tall and wide, and with big wheels. We would drive tanks if they weren't so slow.

From the time a Texan gets that first car as a teen until they pry his old, cold, dead fingers from the wheel, the vehicle is a part of each Texan's soul. Kids start driving when they are quite young. Ranch and farm kids sometimes get hardship licenses at fifteen. These kids have grown up driving tractors and farm trucks. Little ones, who can barely reach the pedals with their toes and still see through the steering wheel, will drive really slow while mom or dad feeds cattle from the back of the truck. After that first heady experience, vehicles become the stuff of dreams. This remains true even through adolescence when boys and girls begin to want to mess around. The vehicle is a make-out haven. Perhaps this is the reason newer truck cabs have been "extended" to the size of small condos. There's a bumper sticker that says, "If you drink, don't park. Accidents cause people."

Basically there are three kinds of trucks: pickups (work trucks), pick-em-up trucks (showy, shiny, sexy date mobiles), and sport-utility vehicles (huge tankers for moms to haul a whole slew of kids). Pickups are battered, beat-up, muddy, nondescript-colored things with bug carcasses embedded in the windshield. You may actually find some tools in the toolbox—that big metal box in the front of the bed. Usually atop that toolbox will be the trusty truck dog. A truck dog, pronounced "dawg," is a venerable animal that lives to hunt, fish, chase cows, and for the golden days when he gets to sit up front next to his owner, who he loves so much he wishes he could open beer cans.

These trucks often have a dried, dribbled, brown stain on the driver's side door, and bumper stickers that declare, "Quit wishin' go fishin'" and "Caution the driver chews tobacco." If you spot a truck with spittin' stains on both sides, you'll know the dawg has learned to open beer cans and has also mastered the art of chewing.

Things Found in the Back of a Pickup (Work) Truck

⋛ ★ ⋚

1) A stack of feed sacks weighted down by a crowbar.

2) One longneck beer bottle with three hand-rolled, smoked-down ciggy-butts inside.

3) Rusty wire neatly rolled and tied, waiting to be recycled as needed.

4) One 17-inch piece of frayed rope, also waiting.

5) One T post remover with a rusty broken chain that can be jerry-rigged if needed.

6) A crumpled *Playboy* magazine dated June 1979, inside a tattered *Cattleman's* magazine cover.

7) Several 2 x 4's in assorted lengths.

8) The rattlesnake assault shovel.

9) Various rusted machine parts that are totally unrelated.

10) The security alarm system—a truck dawg named "Killer" who will protect the truck from "cat" burglars by barking his head off at any cat within 200 yards.

The Other Truck Types

⇉ ★ ⇇

Pick-em-up trucks are a different matter altogether. These are either very new or very old cherry vehicles that are groomed several times a day. Guys carry wallet photos of their polished, big chrome laden prizes to impress the girls. The paint jobs are works of art, with intense colors embellished with racing stripes, sunsets, longhorns, western landscapes, flames, and skies with puffy white clouds. Just showing a girl your classy chassis can be better than foreplay, and can take a lot longer, too.

Truck owners will square off real quick about the best make of truck, and most come down on the side of Ford or Chevy. Entire families are beholden to one or the other, and vehicular intermarriage can cause about as much fracas as a Baptist hooking up with a Catholic.

More recently on the scene is the sport-utility vehicle. Texans took to SUVs right away. They take up both lanes of a highway and at least two parking spaces. Since they don't fit in a normal garage, special jumbo facilities must be built—with a wash bay and half bath, of course. These houses on wheels are tall and wide with room to seat all the Dallas Cowboy Cheerleaders. They are usually filled with screaming cub scouts and often spotted at fast food places. SUVs are specially designed so that their headlights blind you coming and going. If one comes up on you from behind, you might as well cover your eyes and pray. The unique construction includes wide, high bumpers that can cream a normal car from any direction. The driver is never watching the road as her attention is devoted to the banshees in the back seat she is attempting to swat.

There are many kinds of cars, but some will catch your attention and/or your breath. When I came back to Texas, I was shocked to see so many vehicles that in other states are referred to derogatorily as "gas guzzlers." Owners refer to them as that here, but with pride. Cadillacs and Lincoln Town Cars are everywhere. They are heavy on gold chrome trims and are mostly white or black. But there are many with specialty paint jobs matched to the champagne blond of the owner's hair or Aggie maroon or Longhorn orange.

Stayin' Alive While You Drive

≳ ★ ≲

There is a perfectly good reason why we drive large vehicles—it is our first line of defense on Texas streets, roads, and highways. Texas has rules of the road that are not included in the driver's license exams.

★ The obligatory hand signal. On country roads, in neighborhoods, and even on highways and byways in Texas you will notice that the person driving toward you is signaling to you. It is important that you learn these signals and be ready to respond in kind.

The one-finger salute. (It's not what you Yankees are thinking.) If the person approaching you lifts a forefinger from the steering wheel it means "I don't know you, but I recognize that you are a human being heading in my direction on my home turf."

The two-finger half wave. "I see you at the post office and the grocery store frequently enough to know that you must live around here, which is my turf."

The full hand wave. "Hi, ol' buddy. I know you, you old coot, 'cause we went to high school together, and I married your sister!"

★ Forget what you have been taught about four-way stop rules. It doesn't matter if you are on the right, turning, or going straight, if you are female, you go first. Just smile and look at the other drivers, and one of the men will wave you on. Rules be damned.

★ The fastest driver has the right of way. If you are suddenly approached from the rear by a vehicle that appears to be fixin' to mount your trunk, the unwritten law says move over onto the shoulder and drive there until the dust clears or you run into a mailbox. Being polite Texans, when they run you off the road and you are clutching your chest with tears in your eyes, they will wave a thank you.

★ The biggest vehicle has the right of way. Horse trailers, gravel trucks, milk trucks, cattle trucks, or eighteen-wheelers may all pull out in front of you at any time—just because they can. It will take them a while to get up to speed, but don't try to pass, because they only do this in no passing zones. If you manage to get by one, they will pass you and slow down just to mess with you. The drivers get bored on those long hauls of nothing but long miles.

★ When a passing lane is provided, it will invariably be occupied by a very determined senior citizen, who will maintain a steady speed of forty-five miles per hour. Senior drivers fall basically into two categories—those who never leave the shoulder and those who never leave the passing lane. These folks still believe the hype that fifty-five saves lives and gas. They believe they are setting a good example for the younger generation. Our seniors drive until they die, and some even want to be buried in their vehicles. I heard of a man who got his license revoked, but he kept on driving, so his son took his keys away. He hot wired it and kept on driving. His son locked it in the garage, and the old man crawled through a window and drove it out through the back wall and kept on driving. His son sold the car, so the old man got on a riding mower and kept on driving. Still was last I heard. That might be okay, but he doesn't like to drive on the shoulder.

★ Texans do not use turn indicators. We have never cottoned much to giving indications about just what we may do next. That would kinda take the fun out of it. Texans may turn from any lane, at any time—waving and smiling all the way.

★ Speed limits are not to be taken literally except when going through small towns or in school zones. We take those very seriously. Our highway patrol officers are very friendly and helpful. They will listen to why you were speeding—like you needed to get to a bathroom, or you were running out of gas and were hurrying to the fillin' station, or maybe you think you left Jr. at the Wal-Mart, or you just got your nails done and were just trying to catch a breeze to dry them—and with a tip of the hat he will hand you your ticket. Fuzz busters are one answer, but mine goes off for dairies, flea markets, and UPS trucks. I can be sitting at a light next to a patrol car, and the thing doesn't even hiccup. When entering any big city, don't get in the far lane unless your vehicle is equipped with a rocket fuel injector. The closer you get to a city, the faster you have to drive. And stayin' in one lane for more than fifteen seconds is for sissies.

★ Stopping to ask for directions is an entertaining experience to be chanced only if you have plenty of time to fully enjoy it. Whether the individual you approach knows where you are going or not, if male, he will feel obliged to give you directions. His macho manhood is on the line.

"Wall if yew go down here to the main highway where it intersections with the farm road, not the first one now, but the one jest beyond, and yew head west, actually sorta northeast and then it jogs west and head for the highest point, wall then yew'er headin' right toward whare yew'er headed for and then yew cain't miss it." I can always miss it.

Asking for directions in a town is really a joyous comedy of errors, even if folks aren't just messin' with you. Streets all have names, but no one seems to pay much attention to them. Most directions are given according to landmarks. The response to your request for directions will invariably begin with a question.

"You know where the ole Martin place is? Their son, Shorty, used to have the Dairy Queen, he married the Carter girl, and then they moved to Waxahachie? No?"—followed by long pause and scratching of the chin—"well, you know where the Piggly Wiggly used to be before they moved into the old Kmart, when they built that superstore way out from town that's so crowded. You know, where you have to fight your way in, and so big you can't find your way out? No? Well, you know where the First Baptist Church is, that ain't where you're headed, but it'll give you a decent startin' point. You ain't frum around here, right? Well, if you just let me eat my supper, I'll be happy to lead you on over yonder. You come on and join us now. Mom's done het up a chili from Hades that will burn out your eye sockets and leave you bawlin' for more."

Let's Fly Away!

≳ ★ ≲

Now the South Texas heat has been known to make folks crazy, but there's crazy and there's real crazy. We have always wondered if pilots' brains are wired pretty much like bull riders. Back in 1951 some might have questioned the sanity of a former World War II Army Air Corps flight instructor when he purchased a surplus Curtiss P-40 Warhawk. Then in 1957 he sweet-talks four of his buddies into joining him in the purchase of a P-51 Mustang. They each coughed up $2,500 for the plane known as "Red Nose."

So, legend has it that these guys showed up in deep South Texas early one Sunday morning that same year at Mercedes airfield, and some idiot had painted a sign on the fuselage! Much to their consternation the sign read, Confederate Air Force! Did these pilots have the perpetrator arrested and flogged? Heck no, they clinked coffee mugs and agreed that was a mighty fine name for their little group of crazies, and so the CAF was born.

This group of investors bought two Grumman F&F Bearcats for the bargain price of $805 each in 1958. Now they owned (with the P-51) two of the most advanced piston-engine fighters to see service with the U.S. Air Force and the U.S. Navy in World War II.

When the CAF members discovered that many of the great aircraft were being neglected and even destroyed, they made it their mission to recover as many as they could and preserve them. They wanted their kids and great-grandkids to be able to see these magnificent machines for generations to come. They also wanted to make sure that these planes would again fly!

The result of this fine effort has been the American Airpower Heritage Museum. Starting out at Harlingen Rebel Field, the incredible collection was moved in 1991 to Midland, Texas. Here a phased development plan was designed to commemorate World War II aviation.

The museum now houses the largest private collection of WW II artifacts and material outside the U.S. military government museum system. The museum also provides an extensive educational program that includes school outreach and on-site training.

CAF aircraft fly! That sets them apart from other aviation museums. They can go to local communities, appearing before up to ten million folks around the U.S. every year. They teach the lessons of World War II— peace through strength and preparedness.

Although most of the original members of the CAF were World War II veterans, now the youngest colonel (they are all colonels) is only eighteen and the oldest is a mere ninety-seven. The CAF Cadet Program allows teenagers thirteen to sixteen to volunteer during CAF activities, such as air shows, and to be active members of the units. There are many groups around the country.

I have several friends who are colonels in the Confederate Air Force. Colonel Bob, a fine Air Force pilot, recently made a pilgrimage to Midland to the American Airpower Heritage Museum and reported it to be a highly worthwhile experience. He stopped by on his way back home to South Carolina, and that's where I learned about this fine organization and their work.

Bluebonnets and Lady Bird

≷ ⭐ ≶

If ever I so slightly wavered on my decision to make my home again in Texas, my fate was sealed during my first spring back. The queen of the vast Lone Star wildflower dynasty observed her yearly coronation by painting the hillsides and by-ways awash with her white tipped, purple-blue majesty. The hill country display is seductive, and I promised myself that I would be here to celebrate the bluebonnet every year from now until eternity.

The profusion of wildflowers is not totally by chance. Our beloved former first lady, Lady Bird Johnson, took on the beautification of Texas highways and has been an incredible force in conservation and beautification across the country. During the Depression, Mrs. Johnson encouraged Lyndon to establish a plan for roadside parks throughout Texas. He was heading up the National Youth Administration for the state and put the young people to work on the project. Once he was elected president she convinced him to expand her beautification cause, and Congress passed the Highway Beautification Act. She founded the National Wildflower Research Center, which is southwest of Austin. We now boast around five thousand wildflower species—buttercups, Indian paintbrushes, bird's-foot violets, spider lilies, water lilies, Indian blankets, strawberry cactus, and the lush bougainvillea.

The story goes that Lady Bird was driving along one day when she spotted a young man mowing down a field of wild primrose. She pulled over and offered to rent the land from him if he would just promise not to mow down the flowers. This is a woman who saw potential beauty everywhere and made it a reality for the generations to come.

Just remember the bluebonnet rules:

>We can pick bluebonnets in our own yards.

>If your neighbor says you have permission you can pick her bluebonnets.

>Don't you dare pick bluebonnets along state highways because these are considered public property.

>Watch what you are doing when you are posing your kids in the bluebonnets:

>>Don't tromp unnecessarily.

>>Fluff flowers if they get mushed.

>>Watch out for traffic!

Recently the Texas Department of Transportation has discovered a great way to nourish the grasses that keep the slopes along the highways from eroding. It has been determined that a by-product of the dairy industry can be deodorized and sanitized and—yes, we're talkin' cow poo poo!

Texas garden clubs have always been environmentally concerned whether planting trees in parks, tending to drought-threatened public gardens, or bringing flowering shrubs to our inner cities. My mother was an active garden clubber when I was a girl, and one of the first things I did on my return was to join a group in my small town. I was amazed at the valuable work these women contributed to our town—everything from planting trees at the new library to taking turns watering the gardens in the park. Some of our members are well into their eighties, but you would never know it. These clubs are also a good way to get to know your new neighbors.

All of our flowering beauty is not on the ground either. I have been blown away by the fact that so many trees and bushes are flowering, especially since I spent so many years in places where there were so few trees, or they all looked alike.

In Wyoming were I spent many happy years, they practically have funeral services when a tree dies. One early September there was a heavy wet snow that wiped out trees by the dozens where I was living. People walked around with tears in their eyes for weeks.

In California folks pretty much took their tall pointy trees for granted. My cat ran up seventy-five feet in one of those big pines and got disoriented. She was up there for a couple of days while I frantically tried to entice her down with grilled salmon fillets and lobster Newberg. Finally after I had contacted everyone in the phone book, a guy came out who strapped on climbing equipment and crawled up that tree. He bounced all the way back down with Amanda in hand. She never strayed outside again.

I have noticed that most Texas trees seem to be more cat-friendly. I will certainly never take these gorgeous trees for granted. Each one is uniquely formed. As you gaze across the rolling hills, the shades of green vary from a silvery-lime to the deepest emerald. Around here we see a lot of exotic mimosas with their fluffy, salmon-pink blossoms, and crepe myrtles herald the arrival of summer. Pecan trees, magnolias, crabapples, lilacs, redbuds, forsythia, and weigelas abound around the state. From the Piney Woods of East Texas to the cacti and yucca of West

Texas and from the blue spruce in the north to the banana trees in the south, I hope you enjoy and treasure the beauty of our trees.

If you have a mind to check out some fabulous birds, we have them, too. Birding organizations flourish here, and three-fourths of all American birds are represented in Texas. Log on to www.audubon.org and check out the Texas Audubon Society to learn what you can do to save some of our more rare birds. There are seventy-five species that are on the Texas Watch List as being threatened.

Sam Houston State University in Huntsville boasts the Texas Bird Song Library with more than two thousand recordings of birdcalls. The science behind this research is called avian biocoustics. The state's diverse landscapes provide homes for our feathered friends whether they prefer the lake country or the coastline. Birds, bees, flowers, and trees—we have them all!

Growing Pains!

≳ ✶ ≲

If you are planning a lawn and garden for your new home in Texas, you may want to get psychologically tested for masochistic tendencies. Review the weather section, the critters section, and then consider the timeless beauty of a rock garden or maybe painting your asphalt green. Many folks have chosen the latter, saving money on their water bill and trips to their analyst. They generally live next door to a master gardener who welcomes bus tours of school children to their home to tour the flower, vegetable, and herb gardens, all of which flourish.

Actually gardening in the Lone Star State is not as daunting as it may seem at first thought. Texans have led the nation in planting native plants and seeking out compatible species from similar climates. Selecting native or adapted plants is environmentally friendly and will save you a lot of stress. County extension offices, university agricultural departments, garden clubs, master gardeners, and nurseries work together to help novice gardeners have success in all regions of the state. There are also two really good books on "going native" that can help you get started. They are Howard Garrett's *Plants for Texas* and *Native Texas Plants* by Sally and Andy Wasowski.

These sources can help you choose the right plants for your lawn, taking into account sun and shade and ongoing maintenance needs—watering, fertilizing, and the really important mulching.

Then drive around your new town and see what flowers, trees, and shrubs appeal to you. If the owners are working in the yard, stop and ask about what you like. Gardeners like to have their toil complimented. Jot down unknown names and go to the nursery. Folks will be glad to make recommendations about the best plants suited for your area. If you have any problems, contact the local county extension agent for friendly advice. Don't feel your questions are dumb; they have heard it all and are happy to help.

Vegetable gardens do quite well in most parts of the state. In the growing season your new neighbors will inundate you with red-hot chili peppers, green tomatoes, and zucchinis the size of watermelons.

When selecting trees to plant around your new home, choose ones that can survive quick changes in temperature and don't need a lot of water and fertilizer. Trees that have been recommended to me include the ever popular live oak, red oak, lacebark elm, the bur oak, the Texas ash, Texas mountain laurel, the desert willow, and much to my surprise the ginkgo biloba! I thought that was just an herbal brain pill. No, it's a big ol' tree that can reach seventy feet high. (Only problem with it is it stinks. Well, only the female trees with the smelly fruit—so, don't plant those.) Then you can brew the leaves and get smart!

Do check out the display gardens around the state. Fort Worth, Amarillo, Corpus Christi, and San Antonio all have wonderful botanical gardens. The Lady Bird Johnson Wildflower Center in Austin features native plant gardens, both naturalized and formal. The Moody Gardens in Galveston is a must-see with the rain forest pyramid and tropical plant displays. Traveling to one of these attractions will inspire gardeners of any level of expertise. You will go home with new ideas for your own landscape.

Loving Blooms at Yellowrose/Crossroads School

≳ ★ ≲

Madisonville is home to a unique school that teaches children and grown-ups about conservation and the wonder of gardening. This amazing nonprofit organization was founded by my dear friend Miss Bobette. We were roommates at Tarleton State and were as close as sisters. I visited her a number of times over the years and was thrilled by what she has created on her family's homestead.

Bobette started her career as a biochemist, but she loved gardening and wanted to become a master gardener. We often teased each other because she loves to garden (I hate to), and I love to cook (she hates to)—what a team!

When Miss Bobette met Dr. Joe Novak (while she was attending Texas A&M University), he inspired her with the vision of a school that would provide an outdoor conservation classroom. Although she saw the dream as having tremendous value, she had disabilities that were making gardening increasingly more difficult for her.

With her spirit undaunted and a strong faith, she began to plant and nurture the gardens on the family property. Her mother had always taught her that our greatest natural resource is children. The family members dropped suggested names for the school in a hat, and Yellowrose was chosen. The Crossroads comes from the name of the actual town that at one time boomed. Thus the Yellowrose/Crossroads School was born and is dedicated to Bobette's mother.

Miss Bobette toiled in her garden, struggling to do the work that was becoming more difficult with each day. She began to notice that some neighborhood children were watching her and seemed fascinated by the growing plants. They were home-schooled, and their parents were delighted by the prospect of an outdoor classroom where they could learn science in a healthy and happy way.

"I was handicapped, and the kids could do the work I couldn't. Nothing happens by chance," she says. What began with those twelve small-town home-schoolers has become a national success story. Now they have a horticulture 4-H club, twenty-five home-school students, four nearby school districts who visit on fieldtrips, and five surrounding counties who enjoy the educational opportunities at Yellowrose/Crossroads School.

When fieldtrip groups arrive to tour the school, Miss Bobette's students teach the visiting students about the plants, composting, and conservation. The school also provides community service opportunities for folks who have been through the court system. "I not only believe in recycling materials, I believe in recycling people," she says.

The kids love that Miss Bobette has a "bathroom garden" with a sunken bathtub that serves as a water garden and an old toilet with horsetail growing from the bowl and moon vines cascading out of the back. When a wheelbarrow had seen its better days and the rusty bottom fell out, it quickly became a lovely home for geraniums. Pop bottles became bird feeders, and a rusty old bed frame became an actual "flower bed"—nothing goes to waste!

The very best part of this learning experience is that it is so much fun. Each day is a new experience as the students continue to care for the plants and learn what they need. They are taught which plants are native to Texas and their area. They learn that these are the easiest to grow and just how much sun/shade and water each plant needs.

Miss Bobette and her students have developed a butterfly garden, wildflower patch, shade garden, veggie garden, and an orchard. The plan is to have the lush grounds totally filled with healthy plants and paths to follow in order to work, care for, and enjoy them.

Seven-year-old Kristen wrote a letter about what she liked about Miss Bobette's school. "The Yellowrose has fun learning stuff. I wear my old clothes so that I can get dirty, play in the water, and paint. I have lots of fun at Miss Bobette's."

Although Miss Bobette never seeks attention for herself, only for her students and her school, her fine work has not gone unnoticed. She was named Outstanding Conservation Educator for Texas in 1999 by the state Board of Soil and Water Conservation District. She is an exceptional woman, and the children of Texas are lucky to have dedicated teachers like her—my friend!

Head, Heart, Hands, and Health—That's 4-H

≷ ★ ≷

"It's not just cows and cooking," my friend Tedra says. She is an agent for the Texas Agricultural Extension Service and has been involved with 4-H for years. One recent weekend the service was hosting a countywide rally day for one hundred kids. Saturday night was filled with games and activities for youngsters eight and nine years old. "How many teenagers do you know who would give up a Saturday night to work with little kids?" asked another agent. "But just look at how the little ones are looking up to them, like they are movie stars," Tedra said.

4-H is about a lot more than raising an animal, though that is important for some kids, too. One girl who just graduated from high school and got a wonderful scholarship to college likes to brag, "And I never touched an animal!" There are as many opportunities as there are interests. This is a great way for a new student to feel a part of a group quickly and find good role models.

There are cyber camps (computers), sport fishing camps, hydrology camps (that's water), wildlife camps, ranch management camps, and even quail habitat camps. Kids still learn to cook, bake, sew, do arts and crafts, but more importantly they learn leadership and organizations skills that will last a lifetime.

One of Tedra's favorite stories is about her own daughter and a friend she made while at a national convention when they were high school age. Several years later Katherine and her old friend met quite by accident on a flight from Texas to Colorado. The flight landed at Lubbock and didn't seem to be continuing, leaving distressed passengers wandering around the airport. The airline staff made themselves scarce, and the two former 4-H'rs took control of the situation.

They found someone in charge, got the information on what options the passengers had, called the folks together, and organized them into groups according to their plans. "They were simply using the organizational skills they had learned in 4-H," Tedra says.

Students learn how to plan projects by collecting information and using problem-solving skills, the cause/effect relationship, and how to take responsibility for their decisions. They also learn to speak to groups confidently when presenting their projects.

This is also an opportunity for young folks with learning disabilities. "It's hands-on training with one-on-one teaching so they can have great success," Tedra says. 4-H is also open to all people without discrimination. Diversity is celebrated.

"We also get parents involved," she added. "It's not like you just drop them off at school. We have families who have been in 4-H for generations!"

Just call your local extension service office and they will tell you about the groups in your area.

Texas Cowboys

When folks the world round think of a Texan, they have an image of a cowboy in a ten-gallon hat astride a horse. When Texans think of a cowboy, they think of a big, mean lookin' guy wearing a helmet on the goal line for the Dallas Cowboys football team.

There are a lot of real cowboys in Texas who ranch and rodeo and two-step up a storm on Saturday night. Many of them do wear cowboy hats, but we believe you shouldn't call a guy a cowboy 'til you've seen him ride.

Here are some hints on how to spot a real cowboy:

⭐ On work days he's rumpled and covered in doo doo from the bottoms of his rundown work boots to the top of his free-bee cap from the feed store—and he spits.

⭐ On Saturday nights at the dance hall his jeans are pressed with a razor-sharp crease, his shirt is starched, his Stetson is dust free, his dance boots are shined— and he spits.

Most male Texans spit. They all used to chew tobacco—it was one of those unwritten laws. So spittin' is a real cultural thing. Right after a "Howdy, ma'am," and a tip of the cap—they spit. I had a guy miss his aim one time and hit my open toed pump, and then without skipping a beat he asked me to dance.

Cowboys have a great disdain for information that comes from the rest of the country and the world, with the exception of Australia. This is because they have heard Australia is pretty big and Crocodile Dundee kinda looks like one of them—and they are pretty sure they saw him spit.

Rodeo cowboys are easy to spot because they usually have one or more of their limbs in a cast and walk with a limp. Cowboys dress in shirts with snaps instead of buttons and tight fittin' jeans and are always wearing a hat. It never comes off on purpose unless of course they are in church. Their belts are longer than their waist—just in case they need to hog tie something. Cowboys wear silver belt buckles the size of turkey platters, and all of these guys are certifiable. They climb on two-thousand-pound wild animals to get bumped, battered, thrown, and ground into the dirt. Then they run for their lives, jump the fence, flash a dazzling smile from a bloody, muddy face, wave to the crowd, and spit.

Bull riders are to cowboys what top guns are to pilots. They are usually small, wiry guys who hope the massive beast they are riding won't notice they're back there. They mount wild, hell bent behemoths that have been raised for the sole purpose of thrashing cowboys. Baby bulls are taunted with insults like, "Your mother's a cow."

Ladies, don't set your heart on a cowboy, 'cause workin' ones never have any money, and rodeo cowboys never come home from the circuit, 'cept to check their mail. And for gosh and by golly don't fall for a bull rider 'cause his attention span is about as long as a winnin' ride—eight seconds.

Above all remember, as hunky as they are in those tight Wranglers (that make it hard for US to breathe), starched shirts, and smellin' of cologne—they all spit.

Gentlemen, the ladies known as cowgirls are quite another story. They look and smell good all the time, and a little splashed doo doo on them just looks cute. They can ride and rope and ranch with the best, and yet, amazingly, their hair and nails are always perfect. They wear Wranglers so tight they look sprayed on, with cinched tiny belts and big silver buckles won for barrel racing. They can do anything a cowboy can including bull ridin.' I have never seen one of them spit, but I've seen a few spittin' mad.

Let's Go Rodeo!

≳ ☆ ≲

When the time came for the Houston Livestock Show and Rodeo each year, from the earliest I can remember, my family went shopping for appropriate duds. Now understand we were from the piney suburbs of the city, and the only horses I knew were kept at riding stables where we took lessons. But off we trekked in search of hats and boots so that we would blend right in with all the other greenhorns at the rodeo.

If you have never attended a rodeo, you are in for a cultural experience that will assault your senses, starting with your sense of smell. Manure by any other name smells like doo doo. There is a very good reason for wearing boots. But as you stand up for the national anthem and the grand entry with lights flashing and the American flag and the Texas flag sweep into the arena, held high by riders on gorgeous, shining muscled steeds, followed by many more riders in perfectly choreographed lines that circle and cross, creating a pattern of stunning complexity, your heart will swell.

Rodeos actually started as cattle roundups, long ago in what is now Mexico. The vaqueros (Mexican cowboys) began to dare each other to match feats with ropes, horse tricks, or wild bronco breaking.

In the states, rodeos began in earnest in the early 1880s, and there may be some argument about who had the first rodeo. Texans tend to believe that it all started in the West Texas town of Pecos. On Cowboy Christmas (the Fourth of July) cowboys from ranches all around would barrel into town, showing off by roping steers and competing with one another by flaunting their talents. Nowadays the July 4th weekend sees more than thirty rodeos across the country.

One of the earliest and longest running rodeos is the Cheyenne Frontier Days rodeo that dates back to 1872. Apparently a bunch of Texas cowboys arrived in Wyoming and decided to celebrate the Fourth of July by showing off their ability to ride steers. Well, the Wyoming cowboys were not to be outdone, and the competition began to include bronco-bustin' through downtown Cheyenne. Of course in those days there was nobody keeping time and mashing the buzzer at eight seconds. The cowboy just hung on for dear life until he or the horse "give out."

America fell in love with the romance of the western cowboy, and those who lived in eastern cites flocked to Buffalo Bill Cody's Wild West shows as early as 1882. These events included trick riding, roping, bronco busting, and the frightening bull riding.

Now Bill Pickett absolutely invented the sport of bull-dogging when he did it like no other cowboy had ever done it. Wrestling the steer to the ground, he would hold the steer's horns and then wrench his head around and BITE the lip of the animal to control him. There was no other man who could do what Pickett did, but his bull-dogging days ended when a horse stomped him into the ground. He was the first African American to be inducted into the National Cowboy Hall of Fame.

Then there was the youngest bull rider ever—Donnie Gay of Mesquite, who jumped on a bull at the age of three. He became a professional and won eight championships and was the all-time leader in that event. And then that wild man Jim Sharp took the bull riding titles at the National Finals Rodeo in Las Vegas with ten bulls—amazing!

Today rodeos are a business—one that combines show business and sport and is as demanding as any theatrical events in Las Vegas. Appropriately, by the way, Vegas is where the PRCA rodeo finals are held each year.

If your son or daughter wants to get into the rodeo life, they will have to compete in about one hundred rodeos a year. This will cost you. Not only is there maintenance of the horses, but that's tons of money in travel and entry fees. Few cowboys get rich, but some make it big time.

Ty Murray, "King of the Cowboys," who ranches at Stephenville, Texas, holds the all-time winning record of seven, so far, all-around cowboy championships. He has only lost three times since 1989 and was injured those years. His redheaded momma, Joy, was a winning bull rider who swears that Ty's first words were "boo wider." His daddy, Butch, was a horse trainer and recognized his son's talent when he was still a toddler. Murray started riding calves as soon as he could walk and was only nine when he sustained his first injury. A bull threw him and stepped on his jaw. He went on to easily win the national high school rodeo all-around title, the National Intercollegiate Rodeo Association's all-around title, and simultaneously qualified for the PRCA's National Finals where he became the youngest all-around winner at the age of twenty. For the next five years he won the title again until injuries held him out for three years. He returned in 1998 and took the title back. Incredibly, the three events that Murray chooses are the grueling, glamorous ones—bronc, bareback, and bull riding.

Tuff Hedeman won his first world title at the age of twenty-three. He has won a bunch of money and set a record for bull riding winnings with $137,061. He became the first rodeo cowboy to hit one million dollars in earnings.

For most who ride the "circuit" it really isn't the money; it's the life. These folks will spend at least two hundred days a year traveling, not an easy life considering most of the time is in a pickup truck heading for the next rodeo.

Rodeo Events and Terms (So's You'll Know What You're Watchin')

☆

PRCA—Professional Rodeo Cowboy's Association—circuit of PRCA approved rodeos

PBR—Professional Bull Riders tour—45 of the world's top bull riders compete in a 29-event season

NFR—National Finals Rodeo

SADDLE BRONC RIDING—Saddle bronc riding was probably the event that started it all since in the old days bronc-bustin' was a natural function of ranch life. Imagine that you are the rider, surrounded by sweaty cowboys, horseflesh, and FEAR, and encased in a narrow wooden chute. You begin by positioning yourself atop the horse with your feet having to be over the bronc's shoulders, in order to give the horse the advantage—yeah, the thousand-pound animal gets the edge. You then hang onto a rope that is strapped around the horse's girth, with one hand while the other hand must be held high—'cause you can't touch the animal or yourself or the equipment without being disqualified. Your feet must stay in the stirrups, and on top of all of that, your riding style is factored into the score. You've got to look good while your brain is screaming "Mama!" As if that's not enough, you have to hang on, if you can, for the longest eight seconds of your life. You'll have a higher score if your horse is a good bucker, and that means a mean sucker!

49

You are shooting for a perfect score of one hundred points—that's fifty for you and fifty for the animal—only he's not on your team, got it? If you are thrown from the horse, as many are, head for the fence, but don't forget your hat. If you do manage to stay on, a pick-up man will help you off the bucking horse. Oh, by the way, there has never been a 100-point ride in the bronco event, pretty much 'cause if the horse does a perfect job, you will be eatin' dirt.

CALF ROPING—Calf roping is also derived from necessary ranch work, as calves have to be roped in order to be treated. You might think this looks easier and a whole lot safer than bronc riding, so you may want to try it. I'll give you a hint—it's a whole lot harder than it looks. Many a fast and fancy dancing calf has embarrassed a good cowboy. At the NFR in 1995, nobody even qualified, and no winning checks were awarded, so there. The calf gets a head start, and you and your trusty steed chase it. You rope it, jump from your horse, pick it up, and flop it on its side and then tie three of the calf's legs together with a pigging string you have been carrying in your teeth so it will be handy. Having fun yet? Oh, yeah, if you find the calf on its side, you have to stand it up and flop it down again. Once it's tied you climb back up on your horse, who has been keeping the rope taut, and wait to see if the tie holds for six seconds. Right. Easy as pickin' your nose!

BARREL RACING—Although you see women in all events these days, barrel racing used to be the only event where the cowgirls could show off. It's a timed event with three barrels placed in an equilateral triangle. The rider blasts through the gate and makes tight on-a-dime turns around the barrels and out the gate like a flash.

BULL RIDING—Now, if you really want to experience the truest thrill of a rodeo ride, just rub a little rosin on your hands for a better grip and drop down on the wide back of a two-thousand-pound, really pissed-off bull. Your buddies hand you a rope that has been wrapped around this pleasant beast, and then you wrap it back around your hand, anchoring yourself to this mean animal that would just as soon kill you as look at you. Now is when you wonder how your smart momma could have raised a child as "ignert" as you. You nod for your buddies to throw open the gate and off you go.

The rules are similar to bareback bronc riding—one hand, no touching, free hand in the air for eight seconds. The bull may jump straight up in the air, or he may be a "spinner" and rotate in tight circles at neck breaking speed. If you get a real fun bull, he'll do both at the same time, and you can look forward to being stomped or hooked. Getting hooked is just what it sounds like; you are literally on the horns of a dilemma. Since chances are you will be tossed quickly, be glad that the barrel man will be looking out for you. These guys are sometimes referred to as rodeo clowns or bull fighters, but their job is very important—like preserving your life and limbs. These clowns will crawl out of their barrels and distract the bull so he doesn't trample your person and recrease your blue jeans.

Don't be lulled into believing you will have an easy ride if you draw a "muley." Don't underestimate him just 'cause he has no horns; they can be real tough.

Before you take that fateful ride you will want to invest in a vest—a protective jacket that more and more riders are wearing these days. It will hopefully hold your guts in if you get trampled by a bucking spinner. Your spurs are also an important investment. They are not only decorative but assist you in maintaining your balance. Of course the bull loves them, too. Bull rider Michael "The G-Man" Gaffney of Lubbock claims he got his spurs off a buddy for a six-pack of beer. "That beer's long gone, but I still have those same spurs. Every time I get them out of my gear bag, it's like saying hello to an old friend."

BARREL MAN—This guy is also known as the rodeo clown, who hides in a barrel until he is needed to divert a bull's attention in order to protect a fallen rider. Attention! These wild men now prefer to be referred to as "bull fighters." Can't say that I blame them—being chased by an angry behemoth is no laughing matter.

PERFECT SCORE—A rider can score 50 points for not getting thrown and riding with style. A horse or bull is perfect (and worth 50 points) if it gives the rider hell. That equals 100, but it ain't never gonna happen.

PICK-UP MAN—When a rider makes it to the whistle this is the guy on horseback who helps him off.

CHAPS—These are those hot-looking (in all meanings of the word) leather coverings worn over jeans by cowboys. Working cowboys wear them for protection from stickery brush and cactus.

SPURS—Yes, they really wear them. These are the U-shaped metal attachments that fit over the heel of boots and hold a spinning star disk that is used for communicating with the animal. Hello!

RANCH RODEOS—Upon my return to Texas I discovered a marvelous kind of rodeo experience that, although new to me, is older than dirt and a genuine education in real ranching. These are not PRCA rodeos, but real working ranches that put their best hands up against one another in events that happen all over the state in small town arenas.

BRONC RIDING—Similar to the PRCA event with one rider representing each ranch and trying to stay on until the buzzer sounds.

TEAM PENNING—This is amazing to watch as cowboys work together against the clock in order to cut three designated calves from a herd and move them into a pen.

SORTING—You will hear the announcer call a number and a team of cowboys will work together to remove the specific numbered cows in order. Quite a tall order.

BRANDING—Cowboys compete in teams to see how fast they can perform the branding process.

WILD COW MILKING—My all-time favorite event calls for all the team members to rope, hold, and milk a wild cow and carry the proof to the judges. You will laugh and laugh.

Cattle Call For Stars

⸘ ★ ⸴

For years Broadway and movie producers have had "cattle calls" in order to cast their projects. *A Chorus Line* immortalized the painful process in both a Broadway musical and a movie as beautiful, talented girls and boys were putting their best feet forward and strutting their stuff in order to be among the chosen few. Such a cattle call was required in order to cast a project to celebrate Fort Worth's sesquicentennial. The ironic catch was that the starry eyed "wannabees" really had to be cattle—longhorn steers, to be precise.

The Fort Worth herd is comprised of fifteen magnificent beasts, one for each ten years of golden history of this town born on the bluff. The longhorn is featured in downtown Dallas with seventy bronze longhorn sculptures, in fuzzy green topiary in Fort Worth's Sundance Square, and in the Texas Gold bronze next to Billy Bob's, but this was to be a live hoofer performance.

The competition was fierce as the contestants were pared down to just twenty-three. Some excelled in the talent category as Carrot Top did his usual stand-up comedy routine. Curley sang his "My Boy Bill" song from *Carousel* and was a shoo-in as a finalist. Lumpy had a little trouble with the choreography, but stood his ground. Several had an edge since they had toured with the 1995 "Great American Cattle Drive" (from Fort Worth to Miles City, Montana) and already knew many of the routines. Saw (was spelled backwards) the last to make the cut got so nervous he had to take a Prozac. Tex, with his flat horns and name, looked bored with the process as he just assumed he was one of the chosen. Chocolate Chip was afraid that folks would hold the fact that he was from Oklahoma against him, but they didn't. Boss and Blue Gunsmoke tried to encourage the young, wild boys (Rosillo, Tres Zeros, and Diablo) to toe the chorus line. Ned was selected because Curley wouldn't go without him—they have a special friendship. Rancho P. K. and Sancho were included although neither did well in the congeniality rankings.

Most of the movie-star longhorns studied method acting under Happy Shahan of Brackettville. This new batch of talented beauties now perform daily, parading from the stockyards each morning to graze in a grassy pasture and then back to the yards in the afternoon. Tom B. Sanders IV is the lifelong cattleman who teaches the other cowhands about the history so they will be ready to answer any questions that tourists and interested Texans might have. Children will be able to see these magnificent beasts and get to know them by name. They might even get some autographs from the glamour herd.

I made that last part up.

Top Ten Things That Make a Grown Male Texan Cry

⟫ ★ ⟪

10) April 15th and/or the day the property tax statement arrives.

9) The first drop of rain after a two-year drought.

8) A stormy dawn after two straight weeks of rain.

7) Seeing John Wayne defend the Alamo. Again and again.

6) The colors passing in a rodeo grand entry.

5) A steaming hot and spicy bowl of chili.

4) Finding a shady parking space right in front of the feed store for his brand-new pickup.

3) Having a big bird in that shady tree that doo doos on his brand-new pickup.

2) Cheering as the hometown high school team wins state.

1) The national anthem, anytime, anywhere. He may not know all the words or be able to hit all the high notes, but he knows what it means.

Rain-chin'

≥ ★ ≤

If you love getting extremely dirty, living on very little sleep, frequently missing meals, facing death-defying feats on a daily basis, have fingers and limbs to spare, like the weathered look of the Marlboro man, enjoy repeatedly repairing the same equipment, and don't mind being rich on Thursday only to go broke on Friday, may I suggest a challenging career in ranching. First you had better follow around some of the idiots who actually live these lives, if you dare.

Hollywood movies may have romanticized life on the range, but once you have seen it up close and personal I guarantee you will want to sell towels at JC Penney. But if you have always dreamed of having your very own "spread" with some pretty cows grazing in the shade next to a rippling stream while you ride a princely mount named "Prince" in your starched cowboy shirt and jeans, crooning "Back in the Saddle Again," best check out the real world of ranching.

Upon my return to this great state I decided to do just that and called on one of the best ranchers around to ask for guidance. Stonewall "Stoney" Jackson agreed to help me out. Now that's not his real name 'cause he doesn't want to be in the book. So, he's in it. Anyway Stoney told me to come out to his spread and help him feed the next Saturday morning. I was thrilled at the prospect of learning about the ranching business. He warned me that I would need boots, so I bought some real cute ones—red with white stars! I was sure Stoney would be impressed.

I showed up at the appointed hour of 5:30, like before dawn, and Stoney was patting his foot like I was late. He handed me a mug of joe, thick as mud, and said we'd better head for the truck. He set his coffee mug down on the stoop, and I asked if I couldn't take mine since I hadn't finished it. He said, "Suit yourself. I wouldn't." I piled into the grubby work truck with my notebook and camera. As I was balancing my coffee and trying to fasten my seat belt, the truck jolted into gear and Stoney pronounced rule number one: NO SEAT BELTS ON THE RANCH.

As we bounced and jarred our way toward the feed barn, I found I was wearing my thick, still quite warm coffee, and it was effectively removing my makeup. Note to myself: waterproof mascara to be worn on the ranch.

At the feed barn I quickly learned rule number two. While snapping photos I followed him into the fenced pen to feed the horses. CLOSE THE DAMN GATE! ALWAYS—EVERY GATE! As I ran to close it I stepped in some doo doo with my cute red boots. Stoney started to load up bags of feed, and I watched his technique carefully. He simply picked up a bag and swung it onto his shoulder, carried it to the truck, and flopped it into the pickup bed. I grabbed a bag and swung it into the air and it body-slammed me onto the cement floor. The bag that weighed more than I did was torn and spewing its contents. Stoney pulled me off the floor with admonition number three: JUST DO WHAT YOU'RE ASKED. He handed me a broom as I quickly realized the request was implied.

When the truck was loaded and the feed barn floor shiney, we headed out to feed. The sunrise was turning the sky colors I had long forgotten. Stoney had his computer-generated paperwork listing which cows we should find in which pasture. He pulled up to the first gate, and I found out why the no seat belt rule applied as Stoney barked, "Open it." The "please" was implied, of course. Cowboys are very polite, but rainchin' is serious business. Eager to please, I jumped down from the cab and trotted over to the gate. Here I was faced with a large linked chain wrapped around a fat post and hooked on a huge nail. All I had to do was reach around through the barbed wire and unhook it, right? My right forefinger was the first to lose its "Passion Pink" painted nail, and my left thumb was the second. I couldn't really see what I was doing, something was scurrying around in the tall grass by my boots, a fly the size of a helicopter was circling my head, and my scalp was sweating as I heard the truck door open. I thought he was going to save me. "Just push it in a bit," Stoney yelled. I threw my body weight into the gate. As I pulled the chain free the gate knocked me down as it swung open. The truck pulled through, and I started to run toward it, when I remembered rule number two and retrieved the gate. Three more nails were sacrificed, and I made another note to myself: Sign up for weight lifting to build upper body strength.

"Count the cows on your side of the road," he asked. All right, I could still count, I thought. So, he's driving and cows that aren't running from the truck are heading for the truck and crossing the road and playing hide-n-seek behind one another.

"What'd you get?"

"Twenty-three or maybe twenty-four; do I count the calves too? Oh, there's one getting up out of the grass. I didn't see her." Stoney's silence was, well, stony. Rule number four: THE COUNT COUNTS!

Stoney did the count himself by standing in the back of the pickup and turning in a circle. All I had to do was stare straight ahead and be sure no cows crossed behind him. He counted twice and returned to say that we were missing cow #2314. All the cows have little yellow plastic ear-tags with black numbers that match the numbers on the paperwork that also match the numbers permanently tattooed in their ears. This cow hadn't showed up. Stoney fed the hungry crowd and then used his binoculars to look for #2314.

"Well, maybe she's just not hungry today, or she's just taking a nap," I reasoned. I was getting hot and tired and really thirsty, and soon I was going to need the powder room. But off we went to look for her. We drove and drove, and then Stoney would jump out and walk into some thicket and be gone just long enough for me to be sure he was dead. He finally found her down by the stream with a new baby calf half stuck in the muddy bank. I ran stumbling behind him. By the time I got up from falling the third time, he had the baby and momma reunited. Stoney retrieved a large plastic case from the truck and proceeded to tie up the little guy's legs and weigh him. Then I held the cute little white-faced, pink-nosed feller while he got his ear pierced with a tag and a tattoo. Now all he needed was a name—which to my surprise he later got when he was registered. He was stronger than I would have thought, and I was back down in the mud. As I sat watching the baby nursing, I digested ranch rule number five: ALWAYS SEARCH FOR THE MISSING COW!

Another gate, which I opened and closed entirely on my feet, led to another pasture. When Stoney leaned on the horn no one came running. Here we were supposed to find the young bulls, and since they were always hungry something was definitely wrong. We drove along, following the fence into thick forest, and sure enough it was down and trampled flat.

"Those buttheads, those damn buttheads," Stoney grumbled as he jumped from the truck and surveyed the damage. He drove over the downed fence and soon found the rowdy delinquents. Then he herded them with the truck back to the hole in the fence and began to force them through. Parking the truck, he tossed me a pair of gloves.

"You get over on that side, and if one of them wants to wander this way, shoo 'em back." Oh, I thought, I'm going to die right here, trampled by a bull the size of an eighteen-wheeler. One of the monsters looked me over and seeing that I posed little obstacle began to ease in my direction. I waved my arms and yelled, "Shoo, shoo, go back, shoo!" It was the first time I saw Stoney crack a smile.

"They ain't chickens, girl!" He let out a loud howl that sounded kinda like, "Wooooooo Heeeeyahaaaa!" Scared the heck out of me, but the bull just moseyed off to join the others. Rule number six: BULLS AIN'T CHICKENS! I held one end of the fence section up while he patched the other with the rusty wire he kept in little bundles in the toolbox. I noticed that my cute boots were not red anymore, and doo doo and mud plastered my jeans up to my knees. No matter that my grandmother always said, "Ladies don't perspire, they glow!"—I was sweating. With the fence temporarily patched, Stoney filled the feed trough, and we were off to yet another pasture in search of hungry cattle. It was now pushing noon, and I was hot and hungry but primarily in dire need of a pit-stop at the powder room. It occurred to me that Stoney should be needing to find some facilities also.

"No, ma'am, I've taken care of that a couple of times already, but I'll run you back up to the house," he explained as I blushed. Of course, rule number seven: FOR A RANCHER ALL OUTDOORS IS A POWDER ROOM.

On our way back to the main house I shot some photos of the gorgeous blooming cactus plants, the massive spreads of wildflowers, and the lovely stock tanks. Nature's glory was all around us as Stoney slammed on the breaks and spit through his teeth, "You see that thing in the road looks like a fat rope? It's a damn rattler!" He bounded out of the cab, hauled his shovel out of the back, and strode over toward the "rope." In one swift movement he hacked the head off the now writhing snake and with three more blows neatly sectioned it. Finally he chopped off the rattle and carried just that back to the truck. Barely winded, he hopped back into the truck.

"Did you take any pictures of that?" he asked. I sat— still frozen, heart pounding, eyes wide, and hands covering my open, silently screaming mouth. "No? Well, that's too bad, those would have been real good." Rule number eight: ALWAYS CARRY AN ASSAULT SHOVEL!

Finally we made it back to the main house, and I found the powder room post haste. Gratefully relieved, I began to scrub my hands and was startled to find the face of a total stranger in the mirror. I was sunburned and mud splattered, my hair was matted, my shirt was ringing wet, my jeans unrecognizable, and my cute little boots ruined. Amazingly I was smiling and somehow proud of myself as I found Stoney in the kitchen. He offered me an iced tea, which I greedily gulped.

"You want to go check on a calf I got out here in back? She's got no momma, and I'm trying to get one of the other cows interested in adoption but not having much luck."

"You betcha."

"You'll want to grab your camera, she's a cutie."

As we walked out back I could hear that baby crying. When we got to the pen, there she was running after first one cow and then another, desperately trying to latch on. They were kicking her out of the way and ignoring the poor little thing. Rule number nine: COWS CAN BE AS DUMB AND AS MEAN AS PEOPLE.

"Well, this ain't workin' so I'll go fix her a bottle. You want to take a shot at feedin' her?" She had already stolen my heart. "Sure."

I sat with the bottle on the porch steps, and she grabbed that nipple with her pink mouth. Her eyes rolled as she sucked so hard she almost pulled me over. It didn't take long for her to drain that bottle dry. When I got up and walked away, she followed me around trying to wriggle between my legs, nudging me every step or so. I was laughing hard, but old Stoney was bustin' a gut.

"Well, now see there. I was just looking in the wrong place for a momma for her. I'm gonna name that little girl Robinette. She's kinda fancy like her momma."

Well, to tell the truth that was fine with me. We shook hands, and I thanked Stoney for a wonderful day. As I drove down the gravel road to the highway, I decided that ranch rule number ten should really be number one: DON'T CHOOSE THIS LIFE UNLESS YOU LOVE IT!

Texas Females

≥ ★ ≤

The women of the Lone Star State are unique in all the world. We love life and aren't afraid to show it. We laugh out loud and are at the top of our game tellin' a story. More funny things don't happen to Texans, we just think most everything that happens is pretty funny.

A wealthy West Texas lady said she married her husband three times. Waving her diamond laden, perfectly manicured hands, she said she married him the first time because she thought she was in love. She married him the second time because he said he loved her and would die without her. "I married him this last time so I could get it all!"

Texas women are outrageously glamorous and love rhinestones on everything, including denim. We are big into accessories and love jewelry. I know a classy Texas diva named Jane. "That's my name, just plain 'Jane.'" There is absolutely nothing "plain" about this tall, blond beauty who always wears the perfect scarf and rings on every finger and both thumbs. She salts her witty stories with brilliant native phrases, like, "That bathroom's so small you couldn't cuss a cat without gettin' cat hair in your teeth."

To see a whole bunch of Texas beauties at once just tune in to a Dallas Cowboys football game—not the team you understand but the cheerleaders. These gorgeous, talented women wear the tiniest halter tops, little vests, and short-shorts with go-go boots. They do a lot of charity events, perform at all the games, and with a very clean image are role models for young Texas cheerleaders. They

were the first professional cheerleading squad to partici-
pate in a Super Bowl. When owner Jerry Jones took over
the team, he got lots of folks mad by firing the legendary
Tom Landry. But he really teed everybody off when he
wanted to modify the teeny little Cowboy Cheerleader
uniforms. Landry was inducted into the Football Hall of
Fame, and the girls are still wearing short-shorts and big
hair.

There is no classier act in national politics than Texas'
own Liz Carpenter. She served LBJ and Lady Bird in
Washington during his presidency and wrote fascinating
books about her White House years.

Mary Kay Ash rebounded from a divorce to build her
Dallas based Mary Kay Cosmetics business with retail
sales beyond one billion. Now she's helping about
300,000 sales associates to reach their independence.
Texas women know that the best revenge is success.

Former governor Ann Richards is a glam gal who
pointed out that, "Ginger Rogers did everything Fred
Astair did. She just did it backwards and in high heels."
She raised four kids before she stepped into the political
arena. Texas women do it all. They have always worked
side by side with their husbands in ranches, dairies, and
all manner of businesses.

My friend Micky owns a beauty salon where she
spends long days on her feet making ladies beautiful and
then goes home to help her husband with the dairy. One
of her many skills is pregcheckin' cows in the middle of
the night, "Because the girls are calmer then." In case you
don't know what is involved in this procedure, it is not for
the squeamish.

Sandra Day O'Connor, the first female associate justice in the history of the Supreme Court, hails from El

Paso. The eloquent Barbara Jordon from Houston was the first Texas woman elected to the House of Representatives and the first African-American woman from the South to serve in Congress. Kay Bailey Hutchinson of Dallas became the first woman to represent Texas in the Senate.

My friend Kari does all the farming on their place and is never happier than when she is on the tractor. Folks say she looked real cute when she was big and pregnant and drivin' that tractor. When one of her kids fell and cut her head, instead of going to the hospital she just sewed her up. You would never be able to pick her out of the season ticket holders at the Sunday afternoon ballet in the city. Texas women clean up really good

Top Ten Things Found in a Texas Woman's Purse

☆

10) Complete makeup kit stocked with samples from Neiman Marcus.

9) Industrial size can of hair spray.

8) Amazing array of keys to every lock on her property, including gates and outbuildings. Weighs about five pounds.

7) Miniature toolkit with pink handled tools.

6) Roll of duct tape—fixes almost anything.

5) A bottle of Kraft Low-fat Ranch dressing for dipping cheese fries—lunch with the girls.

4) A book with phone numbers of everyone she ever knew.

3) Pocketknife with pearl handle.

2) A small Bible.

1) Oven mitts for driving on a hot day.

Judging Books Without the Covers

When I was invited to attend a "book club" meeting I figured I knew what I'd be in for. I'd belonged to many book clubs in all the other places I'd lived, but this is Texas. A book club, I thought, is like on the *Oprah* show where a few folks get together after reading the same book and talk about it.

No, no, I was assured these clubs had book reviewers. Well, I knew what a book reviewer does. Someone, usually from a city newspaper or a university faculty, selects a few books and tells you whether they are worth your time or not. I knew what to expect now, but this is Texas.

No, no, not really, I was told. I'd just have to experience a "book reviewer" at the "book club." Intrigued, I agreed to attend. Boy, was I in for a real Texas surprise!

I arrived at the PAR Country Club on Proctor Lake at the appointed time and had a heck of a time finding a parking place. I figured there must be some kind of special event going on, like a championship golf tournament or a big charity wingding. I remembered hoping that whatever it was it wouldn't be so loud that we couldn't enjoy our little book meeting.

I was directed to the main dining room and found it packed with well-dressed women sipping coffee and socializing. The tables were tastefully decorated and set to accommodate the assembled crowd. I found the ladies who had invited me, Mayor Kathryn and Betty, and was told that the book reviewer would be one of their favorites, Penny Lynn Terk.

The buffet was announced ready, and the ladies continued to chat while filling plates and finding their seats. I began to ask those around me about the origin of the club and its unusual name—The Rejebian Club.

Some said they were "new" members who had only been coming for ten years or so and referred me to some of the original members. From them I learned that the club was about to celebrate its thirtieth anniversary! The unusual name came from the founder, Mrs. V. Y. Rejebian. I learned that Ermance had been an Armenian from Turkey whose family emigrated to America when she was a young teen. Her family had survived the First World War and the holocaust that had been visited upon her people. She and her family settled in Los Angeles where she attended UCLA and became a teacher in Beverly Hills. After her marriage she moved to Texas, living first in Houston and then in Dallas. Mr. Rejebian, also an emigrant, became a very successful importer of rugs, and the couple became community leaders.

The story went that after attending a rather dry book review, Ermance reported to her husband that she had been a bit disappointed and thought she could do better. He said, "If you think you can do better, then do it." Boy did she ever! She not only became an outstanding presenter but went on to found many new book clubs in the forties and fifties that are still active today.

In the beginning she did all of the reviewing at her clubs and had done the first thirteen years of the club I was attending. Francis, one of the past presidents, said, "She had an extraordinary golden voice that transported us to other lands. She was always dressed impeccably and used no notes, but it was that mesmerizing voice. Nothing could have distracted us from listening. I think there could have been a tornado, and we wouldn't have noticed."

Mary told me that Mrs. Rejebian kind of "blew in on the tail end of a storm!" There was a terrible storm in the summer of 1969, and all of the power was knocked out at the country club. Mary and the ladies who were setting up for the very first meeting were stuck with no electricity. "I called my daughter and told her to bring us some cold drinks. She did, and it was a very good thing, as Comanche suffered quite a bit of damage. But we were just watching it from the club."

Francis remembered that she had been president during the twentieth anniversary. "I called her on the Wednesday before to see if she could make it. She wanted so very much to be here with the club. She reminisced about her dear friends here and really hated to miss the meeting that Saturday. Between the time I spoke with her and the meeting, she passed away." By this time I was fascinated, and as Penny was introduced to enthusiastic applause I couldn't wait to learn more.

The professional actress-turned-book reviewer let us know that she had chosen to review *Love Is a Wild Assault* by Elithe Hamilton Kirkland. She suggested that it was like a Texas *Gone With the Wind* and launched into the amazing true story of a woman's battle to build a life in early Texas. She slipped easily into the voice of the young heroine, and her audience was swept away. Individually we imagined the settings and characters—much as we do when we read a good book. We laughed and got teary as she carefully wove the emotionally spellbinding plot line and neatly tied it up. Unbelievably, an entire hour had passed!

Chatting with Penny after her performance, I found her to be a great source of information. She admitted that her theatrical background had probably contributed to the increase of book reviewers displaying a more "theatrical" style.

"When I came to Dallas almost ten years ago I had attended only one book review, and I thought the presentation was rather like a report and even a bit bland," she said. (I was reminded of the story of Mrs. Rejebian.) She continued, "Well, the first review I gave, the ladies sat there rather stunned as I shifted into first person and actually became the characters. I thought, well I am past the point of no return so let me just get through it, and I'll make a quick exit. Then I noticed them turning to each other and a smile of approval here and there. I suppose you can credit [the rise in dramatic style] to my ignorance initially, and then the acceptance once they recovered from the initial shock!"

She also confirmed my suspicion that this phenomenon was indigenous to Texas. In the materials the local club president shared with me, I came across an article written by Joy Davis, another talented reviewer. In it she told about a journalist who had been dispatched to the Dallas area to write an article about "rich Texans" and stumbled upon the book club circuit. He reported that Texas women were so rich they paid folks to read their book for them! Actually book club members are very well read, but many prefer an educational and entertaining book review to other club choices.

Reviewers are all quite specialized—some do musical presentations, some historical novels in full costume, other do humorous works or are just plain funny. One of the all-time favorites is a ball of fire out of Dallas—

Rose-Mary Rumbley. Interestingly, she claims as one of her mentors none other than Mrs. Rejebian.

Rose-Mary has an extensive background in theatre and film. She has a vibrant personality that fills a room—charisma! She has worked with the likes of "the King of the Cowboys," Roy Rogers, the ever youthful Van Johnson, and that "Kookie" Edd Byrnns from TV's *77 Sunset Strip!* She also appeared in *Paper Moon* in a scene with Tatum O'Neal. It's the final scene when the child is delivered to her aunt's house and decides to stay with her dad. Besides being a talented performer, Rose-Mary is also a writer. She certainly loves her hometown, Dallas. Two of her books that prove it are *The Unauthorized History of Dallas* and *Dallas, too.* She also collaborated on *What! No Chili!*

She told me, "Mrs. Rejebian was like my mentor, and I was so glad to have known her." I found this especially nice because Penny had told me how much Rose-Mary had helped her in getting started. This amazing woman often does as many as three performances a day—driving long distances and arriving on time to welcoming audiences.

I was privileged to hear her review the story of a German who—believe it or not—wrote a history of the Texas Revolution—in German! The book was entitled *Ehrenberg: Goliad Survivor, Old West Explorer: A Biography* and was written by Natalie Ornish. Rose-Mary's interpretation was punctuated by gales of laughter and sighs as the club learned about a man who not only recorded Texas history but also mixed with many notables of the time. He was also responsible for planning the layout of San Francisco. Yeah! The author came across the little book about the Texas Revolution quite by chance and set out to learn what she could about this fascinating man.

Rose-Mary made immediate contact with her audience. Her humor is self-effacing and universal as she manages to find it in almost everything. She also values history and is wise enough to realize that the real history is "in the details" that trigger our memories. If anyone listening to her had ever thought history dull, here's the lady who would quickly change their minds.

I could really visualize Ehrenberg as he emigrated to Texas and became caught up in the fight for independence. I was also caught up in the difference in the quality of this performance from the viewing of a documentary on television.

This experience of having a talented performer interpret a book by stimulating your imagination is precious. I can only hope that this kind of event can continue to survive and even grow as younger folks learn about it and join book clubs—Texas style.

The Lone Star Flag

At the convention at Washington-on-the-Brazos there was some discussion about needing a flag and apparently Lorenzo de Zavala sketched out some ideas: "Rainbow and star of five points above the western horizon; and a star of six points sinking below," with the suggestion that the letters "TEXAS" be placed around the flag. But the first official flag of the Republic was described as "the conformation of which shall be an azure ground with a large golden star central." This, known as David G. Burnet's flag, was adopted on December 10, 1839.

President Mirabeau B. Lamar approved the adoption of a new flag in 1839. This is the Lone Star Flag that became the state flag. Nobody seems to know who designed it, but the flag's colors represent the same virtues as they do in the national flag. Red stands for bravery, white for purity, and blue for loyalty.

THE PLEDGE TO THE TEXAS FLAG

"Honor the Texas flag;
I pledge allegiance to thee,
Texas, one and indivisible."

State Symbols Well Known and Obscure

⋛ ★ ⋚

STATE TREE—The pecan tree was probably chosen because Gov. James Stephen Hogg requested that a pecan tree be planted at his grave. I know you thought it was the mesquite.

STATE FLOWER—You know this one, the bluebonnet. You may not know it is also called the buffalo clover, wolf flower, and *el conejo*, which is Spanish for the rabbit.

STATE MOTTO—"Friendship."

STATE BIRD—The mockingbird, really. They can catch rattlers and peck them to death.

STATE STONE—Petrified palmwood.

STATE GEM—Texas blue topaz.

STATE FOLK DANCE—Square dance.

STATE FRUIT—Texas red grapefruit.

STATE SEASHELL—Lighting whelk.

STATE DISH—Chili, although I have never seen it served in a dish.

STATE FISH—The Guadalupe bass. Worshipped by bass boat owners.

STATE NATIVE PEPPER—The chiltepin.

STATE VEGETABLE—Texas sweet onion—1015s at your Texas market.

STATE FIBER AND FABRIC—Cotton.

STATE FUNGUS—No cheating now, don't shout out the answer. It's the devil's cigar.

In the Beginning

⋗ ★ ⋖

It's no wonder we have so many strange critters in Texas, because millions of years ago this land was a regular Jurassic Park. Back about 70 million years ago when the prairies were covered with water there were giant sea lizards (mososaurs) swimming around with "terrible crocodiles" (*Deinocheirus mirificus*) eating anything they dang well pleased. Big lumbering dinosaurs roamed around Texas enjoying the land along with woolly mammoths, mastodons, saber-toothed tigers, and tiny little horses just over a foot tall. You can still see tracks made by the humongous dinosaurs in the bed of the Paluxy River near Glen Rose. The first Texans came across the Bering Strait during the Ice Age. Prehistoric Native Americans left paintings etched into canyon walls at the Seminole State Historical Park. There are pictographs that date back thousands of years. There is a fossilized reef that arcs up from east of Alpine into New Mexico and dips back down through Carlsbad Caverns National Park and around through Guadalupe Mountains National Park winding up in the Apache Mountains. This has been determined to be the best-preserved fossil reef in the world. It dates back about 250 million years and is about 400 miles long. Where the reef is exposed the high peaks are embedded with plant and animal fossils.

Just north of San Antonio you can explore the Natural Bridge Caverns that were formed from limestone more than 140 million years ago. This awesome underground wonderland of "living" limestone (dripping water continues to change formations) was discovered in 1960, and the natural appearance has been preserved.

As the bow and arrow was designed, the people became hunters, stalking the large beasts and living in protective caves. The climate warmed up, and the inhabitants began to harvest crops and enjoy the bounty of the rivers and lakes. Later the highly civilized Caddos cultivated an agrarian culture and established a complex society.

Many tribes joined the Caddos, and they called each other "tejas" or friends. Other tribes included the Tonkawas, Comanches, Jumanos, and the Karankawas. The Spanish explorers thought the term "tejas" was a tribal name, but these were members of the Caddo Confederacy that ruled in Texas, Louisiana, Arkansas, and Oklahoma. Father Damian Massanet went with the Spanish troops to confront the French, who were in control of the land, and befriended the "Tejas" chief. This was the beginning of misguided attempts to civilize the "savages."

Chief Placido was a Tonkawa who fought alongside early "Texians," as the non-natives were called. He bragged that he had never shed a white man's blood but was thought of as a traitor by his own people. A Comanche chief called Ten Bears lost his leadership role with his tribe for wanting to make peace with the Texians.

The flags that flew over Texas in the early days were: the Spanish from 1519-1685, the French from 1685-1690, the Spanish again from 1690-1821, the Mexican from 1821-1836, and the flag of the Republic from 1836-1845, which became the state flag in 1845. From 1861-1865 the Confederate flag flew as Texas joined the South in the Civil War. The United States flag has flown over our state since 1845 to the present, except for the years of that painful war that ripped the nation, communities, and families.

There was quite a controversy over just where to locate the capital. The Texas government 'bout wore out running from one town to another. They started in Washington-on-the-Brazos but had to escape from Santa Anna and relocated to Harrisburg, and when that was no longer safe, on to Galveston Island. After they had the victory at San Jacinto, the capital was moved to Velasco, and that's where Santa Anna signed the treaties to end the revolution. They didn't stay there either but moved to Columbia, and later Sam Houston moved the government to—where else—Houston, which was named after him after all. When Mirabeau B. Lamar was president the search was on again for a more central location. He found Waterloo and renamed it Austin, and there the capital has remained. Whew!

Texas History
(As Told by My "Gran")

≷ ★ ≷

I learned most of my Texas history at my great-grandmother's knee. As "Gran" would rock and drink hot spiced tea from a china cup, she would regale us with stories of how she came to Texas as a little girl in a covered wagon. Her version of how things happened was a lot more colorful and interesting than what I learned in school—especially when she told of the escapades of a distant cousin, Ol' Cousin Jumbo, "that worthless Cajun big ox, no good, freeloadin' son of a decent momma, who was the only male child born into this family ain't worthy of the name."

I did notice that Gran's stories tended to get ever more exciting with each telling. Some of my cousins thought there might be more in that tea than spice. We sat riveted as she would rock and tell of the time as a little girl that she had hidden all curled up in the cupboard of her house during an Indian raid. The "painted savage" pulled open the door and just looked at her, "so I knew I was to keep quiet." He shut the door and left the family unharmed.

Meanwhile Ol' Cousin Jumbo had run away from his "decent" momma's farm to look for his daddy who had deserted them. Actually, he'd gotten a blister on his "pinkie" finger fixing a fence and thought he'd have a better life in New Orleans.

When he got to the city, he found that folks actually expected him to work for a living. There he met the handsome and brave Sam Houston who was recruiting troops to fight the vicious Santa Anna. Ol' Jumbo looked like a good choice for a recruit since he was taller and wider than all the rest of the men. Fighting didn't appeal to Ol' Jumbo because he thought he might get even worse things than a blister. After Sam pointed him out and asked him to serve, he was soon basking in the glory of the moment and joined the "New Orleans Greys" on the spot.

Up to a point it looked like the Texas farmer forces were cleaning up pretty well as they had easily beaten the Mexican troops at Gonzales and captured Goliad and San Antonio. Ol' Jumbo enjoyed strutting around playing soldier and was looking forward to joining the likes of Davy Crockett at the Alamo. Davy had just lost reelection to Congress in Tennessee and told folks there, "You can all go to hell, I'm a-goin to Texas." Sam Houston sent Jim Bowie to lead the forces at the Alamo.

Santa Anna was ticked off about how things were going, especially when he heard that the Texans had taunted the Mexicans at Goliad with a "come-and-take-it" flag over the cannon. That was on October 2, 1835, and the Texas Revolution began in earnest. Santa Anna knew he could take advantage of the lack of organization in the Texas forces and therefore beefed up the action. He assembled a whole bunch of troops some five thousand strong and prepared to re-enter Texas.

Ol' Jumbo bided his time at the Alamo by making gumbo for the one hundred and fifty troops, while Jim Bowie and Will Travis flipped a coin to see who was gonna be the head honcho. Apparently the coin fell in the stew, resulting in both of them deciding to be boss. This was the beginning of rule by committee, which continues to work just as well today.

Bowie really loved Ol' Jumbo's gumbo and liked to wash it down with sour mash. When Santa Anna showed up on February 23, Jim was in the kitchen doing just that. Travis hollered for him to look out the window as there was a blood-red flag hoisted high, meaning no quarter, no surrender, no mercy. In an unprecedented show of unity, Bowie and Travis signaled the cannon, and the siege of the Alamo began.

The Mexican troops surrounded the Alamo and began bombarding immediately. Travis quickly called for a strategy meeting, but Bowie had to beg off with a stomachache. Ol' Jumbo took what was left of the booze and played cards with Moses Rose. Now Moses knew from battles and defeat, as he was a veteran of Napoleon's retreat from Moscow. He had a plan to vamoose if things didn't improve soon. The relentless assault continued for days. Jim Bowie called Ol' Jumbo to his sick bed and said, "If I live through this bellyache, I'll gladly demonstrate my Bowie knife on your guts."

About that time Travis called all the troops together and told them that the situation was pretty darn dire. He drew a line in the dirt with his sword and said if they were prepared to die for freedom they should cross the line; if not, they'd better just get out. He had written a letter to the people of Texas in which he had stated, "I shall never surrender or retreat... I am determined to sustain myself as long as possible and die like a soldier who never forgets what is due to his honor and that of his own country—Victory or Death." They all crossed the line—even Bowie got carried across—and said they'd fight to the finish, except for Moses and Ol' Jumbo who crawled out on their bellies in the dead of night.

At dawn on that fateful morning of March 6, Santa Anna and his men attacked full force. When the fight was over all of the brave Texans were dead. When the news finally reached across the territory, proud Texans rose up spittin' mad and ready to give Santa Anna what he deserved—death.

Ol' Jumbo had crawled backwards on his yellow belly through the enemy lines mumbling to the Mexicans, "¿cómo te va?" When he saw troops no more, he ran, and he ran, and he swam, and he swam down the San Antonio River.

Sam Houston left the convention at Washington-on-the-Brazos the very same day that the Alamo fell. He headed directly toward Gonzales to organize the Texas troops. A Mrs. Dickinson and two slaves showed up at Gonzales and told of the horrors of the Alamo. Sam told James Fannin to leave the old presidio in Goliad and retreat to Victoria. About this time Ol' Jumbo stumbled up to Fort La Bahia and offered to cook some Jumbo's gumbo for Fannin and the troops.

Ol' Jumbo claimed he struck up a friendship with Fannin, and they ate gumbo and shared shots of whiskey, flipping coins—"Heads we leave, tails we stay, two out of three, heads we . . . " Finally the troops moved out, but the Mexicans confronted them on a wide open prairie. After a brief fight, Fannin surrendered, saying he had a stomachache. Jumbo's gumbo strikes again.

Santa Anna issued orders to execute all of the prisoners, and they were marched out of the fort believing they were being transferred. Ol' Jumbo might have been dumb as a bar ditch, but when he heard the gunshots and screams, he figured out fast enough where they were being transferred to; and he ran, and he ran, and he swam, and he swam, and he ran some more. About three hundred and fifty Texans were not so lucky.

Houston, meanwhile, was organizing the Texas troops at the San Jacinto River, just waiting for Santa Anna to do something stupid. Ol' Jumbo joined up with Erastus "Deaf" Smith and his scouts. He learned some tricks from Henrick Arnold, a free black who was a valuable spy for Houston.

By this time the troops were more than ready to get it on with the Mexican forces. They were madder than hell and tired of waiting around. Then the word came that Santa Anna had moved his troops directly in front of the Texas position—the time had come.

Houston rallied the troops saying, "When you engage the enemy let your battle cry be Remember the Alamo!" The cry went up, "Remember the Alamo!" Thomas Rusk added, "and La Bahia!" The cry went up, "Remember Laberde!" because that's what they thought they heard. Because some knew where it was, they yelled "Goliad." So they charged into battle with these war cries. Everyone knew what the point was; the point was to avenge all the brave Texans who had died.

There were old men and young, seasoned warriors and kids off the farm, but Ol' Jumbo was not among them. There was an old man who brandished two guns because he had lost his son and his son-in-law at the Alamo. One of the captains was Jesse Billingsley, a tough cookie who wore buckskin and was known to sleep on the floor. When the Mexican army began their afternoon siesta, Billingsley waded his men into battle and heard the Mexicans begging, "Me no Alamo." Houston sent word to him at the front to slow down as surrender was imminent. The captain's reply was, "Present my compliments to the general," he paused, "and tell him to go to hell." His troops swept on victoriously, and the battle was all over in less than twenty minutes. But it took Houston quite a bit longer to call off his men.

Ol' Jumbo was hiding in the tall grasses as always, on his belly, when he noticed a grubby Mexican soldier. The soldier offered the Cajun a bunch of pesos to help him escape. He looked as if he could make good on the deal as he was wearing a silk shirt under his grody jacket. As Ol' Jumbo was considering the possibility, another Texan approached. The big oaf jumped up, pulling the Mexican to his feet, and proudly marched him back to camp. Upon seeing him, the other prisoners greeted him with cries of *"El Presidente."* Ol' Jumbo was a hero, and Santa Anna surrendered to a wounded but proud Sam Houston—the Republic of Texas was born.

Skirmishes with Mexico continued as first Sam Houston and then Mirabeau B. Lamar served as presidents of the Republic. War reached a high pitch in 1842 when the Mexican army took San Antonio and declared the reconquest of Texas. Volunteers banded together; among them was the now acclaimed Ol' Jumbo—the man who captured Santa Anna. Against his will, he was rushed along by the fervent troops who were eager to drive the Mexicans from their land. These gallant troops were successful and chased the Mexican forces back to the border. Some of the men decided to continue the chase. On Christmas day they attacked the village of Mier, only to be squashed by a force that outnumbered them ten to one.

The Texas prisoners were marched to Mexico City, and Santa Anna—yeah, he was still there as Houston didn't off him when he had the chance—ordered them executed. During the march, the Texans tried to revolt but were recaptured and told that one in ten would be executed. They had to draw beans from a pot, and the ones with black beans were to be shot. Ol' Jumbo palmed a handful, presented a white bean, and choked down the rest. Once again he slipped through death's grip, like a weasel through a knothole, while brave men died.

The remaining men were marched on to the castle of Perote and imprisoned there. Ol' Jumbo was put to work in the kitchen where he befriended a man named Henry Journeay, a brilliant carpenter who worked in the wood shop building a chair of state for Santa Anna. Ol' Jumbo brought soup bones from the kitchen. Journeay saved bits of wood from the shop and with a stolen file created—amazingly—a violin.

An escape plan was devised: As Journeay played the violin, the other men dug their way to freedom. When they heard the guards approaching as they were unlocking the many bolts on the heavy doors, they hid the violin. It was never found by the guards, and thirty-two prisoners crawled to freedom. The others, including Journeay, remained for two more years. Ol' Jumbo had sucked in his fat gut and squeezed out at the first opportunity.

Sam Houston, that handsome man as Gran would say, was in his second term in 1844 when he restarted negotiations for annexation with the United States. James K. Polk, who had won the nation's presidency on a platform of westward expansion, supported Houston's proposal. On December 29, 1845, the U.S. Congress accepted the state constitution, and Texas became a part of the United States.

As one would expect, a lot of political wrangling occurred between the 1836 Republic of Texas and the 1845 State of Texas. Houston started negotiations with the U.S. almost immediately after gaining independence with Mexico. Finally in March of 1837, President Andrew Jackson recognized the new country. Lamar, who replaced Houston as the president of Texas in 1838, opposed annexation because he had visions of grandeur for the new country. He established contact with Great Britain, which caused much dismay in the U.S. Congress. Sam Houston was reelected in 1842, Jackson had been replaced by Tyler, and now Polk was president. Now Texas could become a state like all the rest—no, of course not.

In 1844 Texas and the U.S. signed a resolution to annex Texas as a territory. The Senate rejected the treaty. In February of 1845 Congress approved bringing Texas in as a state. Texas was allowed to keep its public lands but made to retain its public debt. Anson Jones, who had replaced Houston, called a convention, and the state constitution was written. The annexation terms allowed Texas to split into four additional new states. The questions now arise: Can Texas have eight more Senators or can it de-annex and be a separate country? Politics, like everything else in Texas, is bigger and stranger than anywhere else.

Ol' Jumbo retired from his distinguished military career and lived out his days in Galveston, making gumbo and regaling folks with his heroism. But Gran always knew the truth: "He was a worthless Cajun, big ox, no good, freeloadin' son of a decent momma!"

Texas Rangers (The Originals)

My great-granddaddy was a Texas Ranger, and this was always a source of great pride for my whole family, especially Gran. Of course the fact that he left her with a farm to run, seven kids to raise, and very little money wasn't ever mentioned.

The Texas Rangers were formed in 1823 by Stephen F. Austin, the Father of Texas, for the purpose of covering the vast areas of west and south Texas to protect his colonies from renegade bands of Indians. They also confronted bandits, horse thieves, cattle rustlers, stagecoach and train robbers, murderers, and all assortments of lawbreakers.

A prospective member would be expected to be able to ride, shoot, and cook. Once chosen, a Ranger had to learn to ride like a Mexican, trail like a Comanche, shoot like a Tennessean, and fight like the devil.

That was a tall order, and according to historian T. R. Fehrenbach, "Rangers, born of the frontier, embodied many of the bedrock values of the frontier. They were brutal to enemies, loyal to friends, courteous to women, and kind to old ladies." They were also known to "shoot first and ask questions later."

My Gran loved to tell the story of a small town in West Texas where a riotous mob was wrecking everything in sight. The mayor sent for the Texas Rangers but couldn't believe his eyes when one solitary Ranger got off the train. "They only sent one Ranger?" he asked. The

Ranger tipped his hat and replied, "You only got one riot, right?"

One young man, Tom Sieker, related his story in the *Dallas News* in 1929. He was still living with his parents in his home state of New York but wanted to join his brothers who had moved to Texas and joined the State Ranger Service. Having no idea what the ranger life would be like, he set out for Texas.

"I saw my first Indians and prairie chickens [on the way to Austin]." He made it to Austin and put up at the Kingsbury Hotel, which had a connected wagon yard. People warned him not to go any farther west. The population out that way, they said, consisted of rough customers who took their meals with a Winchester across their legs and a six-shooter on the right side of their plates. He met a man named DeLong who knew his brothers at Fort Mason and was headed that way. "We set out early one morning. I rode in the rear wagon with him. When we had proceeded about seven miles, the driver of the forward wagon suddenly leaped up, and clapping his hand to his stomach yelled 'Tarantula'!"

Young Sieker thought the poor man had been bitten and wanted to run to his aid, but DeLong took his time. When they made it to the front wagon, the "bitten" teamster had bored a hole in a barrel of whiskey, inserted a straw, and was sucking the booze through it. "In his disengaged hand he clutched a bunch of straws, which he offered us." He soon realized that the cry "Tarantula" was the signal that it was high time for a drink.

The next day they stopped in Fredericksburg and stayed at the Nimitz Hotel. "The German settlers there had just lynched a prominent member of a band of cattle thieves, and the band was breathing threats of revenge." Quite a welcome for the future Ranger.

He told of bacon boxes that were maintained along the lines. "Any wayfarer was welcome to eat his fill out of such boxes but was expected to not carry anything away with him."

"There were bad men in the West in those days. These were men who had branded more cattle in an irregular way than custom allowed and were outlawed. Once I drifted into an eating house at Scabb... and found myself in front of eight of these [outlaws]. Each one had a Winchester across his legs and a six-shooter by his plate. In such a chance meeting, a Ranger always bowed and said, 'Well, boys, too many for me,' and in turn, the outlaws would bow and smile pleasantly, and nothing more would come of it."

Walter Prescott Webb wrote, "Surely enough has been written about men who swagger, fan hammers, and make hip shots. No Texas Ranger ever fanned a hammer when he was serious, or made a hip shot if he had time to catch a sight. The real Ranger has been a very quiet, deliberate, gentle person who could gaze calmly into the eye of a murderer, divine his thought, and anticipate his action; a man who could ride straight up to death."

Speaking of guns, Captain Jack Hays sent Samuel H. Walker to New York to help Samuel Colt redesign the Colt handgun to meet the needs of the Rangers. A gun that didn't have to be dismantled in order to reload was needed for the new style of fighting the Wild West required. That gun, with a longer cylinder, became known as the Walker Colt.

Once again in 1846, Hays, now a Ranger colonel, sent Walker to make a thousand pistols so each Ranger would have two. Colt had seen bad times, going bankrupt a few years earlier, but he designed another gun known as 'The Old Army' and had the Whitney Gin Company make them.

Captain Jack Hays was known as a fearless fighter who befriended the Lipan Indians and one Chief Flacco in particular. They waged many successful campaigns, but one was quite memorable. Equipped with only a small party, they encountered as many as one hundred Comanches. As Captain Jack was contemplating how to best extricate the group from an untenable situation, his horse spooked and ran away with him—directly into and through the Indian forces. Chief Flacco thought he was charging and followed him. The Comanches scattered. Later the chief said, "Captain Jack heap brave man, not afraid to go to hell by himself."

Chief Quanah Parker, son of Cynthia Ann Parker and Chief Peta Nacona, was a tough adversary for the Rangers. Once he and a band of braves stole a herd of horses. When he was caught by the Rangers, they told him he would have to tell his two lovely wives that he could only keep one of them. The chief thought a moment and responded, "No, you tell 'em!"

The Texas Rangers made their share of mistakes. Some Indians and Mexicans were mistreated, but on the whole, the frontier was a far better place because of their strong presence. Sam Houston said, "You could withdraw every regular soldier from the border of Texas if you would give me but a single regiment of Texas Rangers."

Famous Texans You Should Know

David "Davy" Crockett was one of those Texans who got here just as soon as he could and had only been in the territory less than six months when he fought and died at the Alamo. He heard about the war with Santa Anna and headed straight for San Antonio. He met with Colonel Travis and said, "I have come to aid you all that I can in your noble cause." He more than earned the right to be a Texas hero.

Stephen F. Austin is known as the "Father of Texas." This educated man of vision quickly saw the potential in this land while it was still uncharted and a Mexican territory. He led the Anglo colonization of Texas.

Samuel "Sam" Houston led the army that freed the Texas region from Mexico. Houston then served as the Republic of Texas's first president. When Texas became a state, he served as a U.S. senator from Texas. Later he became governor of Texas.

Jose Antonio Navarro was the only native-born Texan in the assembly that wrote the Texas Constitution. Of Spanish descent, he held several positions in the Mexican government but stood against Santa Anna and for Texas independence. He was condemned to death but later escaped to Texas where he became an advocate of Texas statehood.

Cynthia Ann Parker was kidnapped by the Comanches as a little girl and was recaptured by frontier soldiers when she was thirty-four. By then she had totally accepted the Comanche way of life. She was married to

Chief Peta Nacona and had two sons and a daughter, Topsannah. She was miserable in the white world, and her white family would not let her go back to the Comanches. When her daughter died, she lost her mind, starving herself to death. Her son Quanah became a chief, and his hostility toward whites was fueled by his mother's suffering.

Jane Long "The Mother of Texas," was left by her husband at a fort near Galveston when he decided to go to Mexico. The fort was vacated, leaving a pregnant Jane, her six-year-old daughter, and a young servant girl to wait for her husband's return. Over a long and unusually cold winter, she gave birth and single-handedly headed off an Indian raid by firing the fort's cannon.

Henrietta King started her married life in a small adobe hut and wound up owning the 600,000-acre King Ranch. Some said she was so tough they would rather "tangle with the Captain than with Henrietta." General Robert E. Lee was a close friend and one of the many rich, famous, and poor who knew of her hospitality. Ranch workers called her "Little Mother of Kingsville" because of her kindness and concern for them.

Quanah Parker was a Comanche chief who fought to keep the Anglo settlers out of Comanche territory. He became a great leader in farming and education.

John Nance Garner, born in Red River County, was Franklin D. Roosevelt's vice president. He returned to his ranch in Texas where he lived to be ninety-nine.

Dwight David Eisenhower, born in Denison, became a general and led the allied army in WW II. He was elected president of the U.S. in 1952.

Lyndon Baines Johnson, born near Stonewall, was a congressman and then a senator from Texas. He became John F. Kennedy's vice president and then president upon Kennedy's assassination.

Oveta Culp Hobby, born in Killeen, founded the Women's Army Corps and served as the secretary of health, education and welfare.

Barbara Jordon was the eloquent first black female senator from Texas.

Babe Didrikson Zaharias, born in Beaumont, was the world's greatest woman athlete and Olympic gold medallist.

Dan Rather was from Houston, started KPRC, and moved on to host the *CBS Evening News*.

George W. Bush was governor of Texas and probably president by the time you read this.

Real Texas Sportsmen/ Sports Without Balls

≥ ★ ≤

True sports in Texas involve fire, firearms, or water deep enough to drown in—and booze. When good ol' boys set out early for a day of huntin' or fishin', their first stop is the liquor store. There they lug in an Igloo cooler as big as a casket and pack it with enough beer to get an entire college fraternity through a weekend.

Hunting is a noble sport, almost a religious experience with all the things a real Texan loves—being close to nature, wildlife, comradeship, and guns. Texans love guns. They hunt big wild things and little bitty feathered and furry things and, of course, Bambi.

On opening day of any hunting season, non-hunters don't even bother to get in their vehicles because traffic through any small town will be tied up most of the day. Bumper to bumper with full gun racks and enough ammunition to start a war, they head out in their trucks for their hunting leases on big ranch spreads, set up camp, start fires, and get drunk. The next morning, they dress in survivalist gear and climb into little towers painted camouflage to fool animals into believing they are seeing a tree with four trunks. They stalk through the bushes making weird calls to flush out dumb birds like turkeys so they can shoot them. If they actually find a turkey dumber than they are, which is highly unusual, they pluck and clean it, fill a drum barrel full of oil, and deep-fry that sucker. All recipes I have seen for this procedure caution against drinking during this preparation. All deep-fried turkeys I have tasted were prepared by drunks.

Fishin' is probably the biggest participation sport in Texas. It is the only sport you can do sitting down and drinking. Oh, I forgot bowling, but that requires balls. Folks fish in lakes and ponds and rivers and the Gulf and tanks. Tanks are man-made ponds for cows to enjoy, but most owners keep them well stocked with fish. Cows don't care much for fish. 'Cept maybe a long time ago when Judge Roy Bean, the "Law West of the Pecos," was accused of watering down his dairy's milk. He explained there were minnows in the milk because the cows were drinkin' from the Rio Grande River.

Texans like to catch all kinds of fish—catfish, perch, crappie, gar, or anything with a fin, but probably the all-time favorite fish is the large-mouth black bass. This fish has a cult following. These folks don't have plain ol' fishin' boats—they have BASS BOATS. Bumper stickers on pickups read, "My other car is a bass boat." There's a sign in a seafood restaurant in Corpus Christi that reads:

> Wanted
> A good woman
> Should cook and sew
> And wash and iron.
> Must own a boat and motor.
> Please send picture
> Of boat and motor.

A gentleman by the name of Gary told me the story of a lady who showed up at her local newspaper office to report her husband's demise. She was known around town as quite a skinflint. When she learned that she would have to pay a dollar if the notice was over seven words, she said, "Just say—John Brown died." The editor replied, "Well, ma'am, you still have four more words free." The woman said, "Then add—bass boat for sale!"

Contrary to popular confusion, the new Bass Performance Hall in Fort Worth has absolutely nothing to do with large-mouth bass, although a bass may join a tenor or soprano in an opera on its stage from time to time.

If you are among the bass lovers, you will be thrilled to know that a huge shrine has been erected in Grapevine, Texas, devoted to your favorite fish. The Bass Pro Shops Outdoor World offers 200,000 square feet of more than everything your little heart could ever desire. All outdoor equipment for fishing, camping, and hunting at one location. It don't get better than that!

My Uncle Phil used to say he tried to quit fishin' one time and joined Fishermen Anonymous. He said if he got a real need to go fishin', he'd call FA, and they'd send some good ol' boys over to help him get drunk.

My nephew, Rob, went fishin' recently and called me all excited to tell me about his adventure. I asked him if he caught a fish and he said, "Yeah, but that wasn't the best part." He was swatting at a mud dauber that was dive-bombing his head and caught his finger on a lure he'd stuck in his cap. The hook had pierced his finger. "Then I saw I had a big fish on the line, and Mom was freakin', and I went ahead and pulled him in, and then we went to the emergency room. It was cool." He's on his way to learnin' fishin'—like not stashing lures in your cap—and just plain ol' having fun.

Fishin' Texas style is a psychological procedure. It may look like there is not much going on, but the fisherman must psyche-out his opponent—the wily, silvery prey that can disappear faster than double-struck lightning. Some men have tried hypnosis—swaying slowly and counting backwards from a hundred. The problem with this technique is that the stalker can succumb to the trance and fall out of his boat. And then you've got those snakes to contend with.

DISCLAIMER—There are lots of folks who hunt and fish and follow the rules. They just aren't as funny. To get your license by phone call 1-800-TX LIC 4 U (1-800-895-4248) 24-hours/day, with approved VISA or MasterCard.

The Reason for the Season

Growing up in Texas I was, of course, a big football fan. Many of my fondest memories revolve around the game. Thanksgiving weekend was marathon football. Dad would pull both of the TVs into the living room, and we would watch every game, with the A&M/Texas match more central to the holiday than the turkey. Texas A&M Aggies and University of Texas Longhorn fans have more animosity for each other than do liberals and conservatives. Longhorn fans try to burn down the Aggies' bonfire, and Aggies have been known to steal the famous Longhorn steer mascot. The game's outcome awards the winner bragging rights for the coming year. Having no family allegiance to either school, I always pulled for the underdog.

As I went out into the world, I felt out of place when women would complain about their sportsaholic husbands. I was always a bit concerned if a man I was dating politely stated a TV preference for vintage movies over sporting events. Faintly smiling, picking at my tofu and seaweed, I'd long to be sitting in front of a big screen with a burger/fries combo at a good sports bar, screaming at the top of my lungs, "Kill 'em. Break his knees!"

Upon my return I was thrilled when a "real man," Buck, a native Texan, asked me to go to a football game. He arrived at dawn in his shiny pick-em-up truck with the toolbox filled with provisions, and we headed for the city. As we neared the stadium, the traffic slowed to a snail's pace, and he entertained me with the stats on all of the starting players. We passed folks sitting in their front yards next to signs that read, "Park Here $50." Buck confidently pulled into the vast parking lot ignoring the "lot full" sign and drove up close to the front where his ol' buddy Tiny, who was 6'5", 300 pounds, had his SUV parked sideways, taking up three spaces.

"Anybody mess witcha?" Buck queried.

"Do I look like a girl?" Tiny laughed, then spying me added, "Sorry, ma'am," and spit.

I got out of the truck as the two drivers jockeyed their vehicles into the outside spaces creating a "stadium patio" with the smoker/barbecue in the middle. All radios were tuned to the pregame show while folks came by to visit, share coffee, and psyche themselves up for the big game. The parking lot began to look and feel like an RV rally. The radio announcer described how the highly paid coaches were yellin', arm flaylin', and pacin' in the locker rooms, like fire and brimstone preachers whipping the teams into a frenzy. I became quickly aware that I was the only one around not sportin' the team colors. Buck was assuring folks that I was not a spy for the other team, so when the sweatshirt hawker came by I bought one. I pulled the sweatshirt on over my outerwear, as this was one of those three cold days I warned you about. After consuming smoked turkey legs and bowls of chili, we closed camp to join the hysterically screaming fans inside the stadium. But first Buck and Tiny had to use the truck mirrors to paint their faces. They butted heads, growled, bumped bellies, handed out earplugs, and since the vehicles were locked, I had no choice but to follow them into the stadium.

No big deal you say? The NFL is like that everywhere? This was not the Super Bowl, no, no, not even college ball. No, this was a high school state play-off game. I was back in Texas where football is the reason for the season!

As I mentioned in the introduction, football is religion in Texas and that being so, Friday is the football Sabbath. On fall Friday nights and Saturday afternoons around the state, you will find stands filled with dedicated fans wearing the school colors, screaming at the refs, chanting cheers, clapping, booing, and creating a deafening roar by shaking coffee cans filled with ball bearings—not just students, no, most of these folks are "grown-ups." They know all the players by name and can quote stats and predict plays. These folks will fill buses to the playoff games if their team makes it. They paint their downtown business windows with "win" slogans and listen to the coaches' weekly radio shows at work. If they have ever had a kid actually on the team, they are local celebrities, but most of them haven't. Their kids are long gone, and there they are "just s'portin' the team."

The frequent state 4A champion Stephenville Yellow Jackets fans have developed state-of-the-art racket making. Fanatic fans have found larger containers for their noisy ball bearings using empty oil paint buckets, propane tanks, and even a rotating oil drum. Obviously it's working for them with three crowns in a six-year span.

Football season in Texas begins in August (crowds show up to watch the practices), goes on through the fall, but doesn't end with the playoff games. We also have spring football, 'cause we cain't live without it for long. The large majority of all games are played in scorching heat. I remember my college days when going to a game meant standing in the heat, sweating out a stylish fall ensemble, makeup melting, hair frizzing, and my left shoulder numb and sagging under the fifteen-pound weight of a vastly ribboned, triple mum corsage the size of a casket floral spray. Amazingly mums are still in vogue, and Lord knows the heat hasn't let up.

Imagine the great fun the players are having poised at the line of scrimmage, with feet, ankles, knees, elbows, wrists, shoulders, and any other injured or potentially vulnerable body part wrapped, taped, and padded as they peer through nose guards, dripping sweat, and trying to hear plays through helmets over the deafening roar of the crowd. So close they smell each other's fear as they lunge into the fray, attempting to survive the hellish heat that flirts with the 100-degree mark. Truly this is a sport that could only have been "made in America" and perfected in Texas.

So, if you want your son to have this character-building experience, plan to live in a district with an outstanding program. You can usually determine this by the head coach's salary. If he is paid more than the combined salaries of the faculty and staff, that's a good sign. If the school has a state-of-the-art stadium, weight rooms, and locker rooms with Jacuzzis and saunas, consider the program. If the uniforms come with little "swooshes," hire a personal trainer for the kid and sign up for the program.

Concerned that your daughter will be left out of the spotlight during the season? Fear not! She can be a cheerleader, twirler, or on the dance/drill team. Texas is famous for beautiful, talented girls who master complex choreography worthy of the Rockettes. They perform (in costumes that would make Bob Macky proud) at all sporting events, in parades (you have probably seen the Kilgore Rangerettes), and along with the Dallas Cowboy Cheerleaders at special half-time events. But like your son, she will need to be groomed and trained. Gymnastics and dance classes will be necessary along with a separate bank account for costumes. Don't forget to factor in the lawn signs with your kids' names. These come painted in the school colors with the mascot so folks can be jealous and the tour buses will know where to pull over for autographs. I made up that last part.

Big schools have big programs with great facilities and equipment, but even little schools have six-man football teams that compete just as fiercely. Gordon High School's Longhorns are famous, having been featured on ESPN and in *Sports Illustrated*. The town has a population of four hundred and sixty-five, but the stadium seats 2,500, which isn't enough when they play a grudge match with neighboring Strawn. And these small schools need cheerleaders, right? Texas football training starts early with little tikes bashing one another in Pee Wee games. They wear giant helmets and pads and are egged on by tiny little cheerleaders in beensie teenie little costumes that are exact replicas of the city high school cheerleaders. Little girls go to cheerleading camp and little boys go to football camp—parents can't even afford to camp out.

If you haven't managed to get your kids into a winning program, but they are really good, all may not be lost. I have heard that districts interested in recruiting a talented player will do just about anything to get him. The family of one such young man, who lived just outside a devoted school district, came home from vacation to find their house had been dragged across the county line. All's fair in love, war, and Texas football.

If you are not a big football fan, fall Friday nights are good times to go out to eat or shop at Wal-Mart, 'cause you'll have the whole place to yourself.

I attended a small college (now not so small, Tarleton State University) that is a part of the Texas A&M system while my boyfriend attended UT. My allegiances were torn, and the joyfully remembered Thanksgiving holiday games of my youth became for me dreaded events to be avoided at all cost. Across the country there are many celebrated, long rivalries between colleges, and yet none is more intense and at times vicious than the bitter conflict that has raged since 1894. If you are coming to Texas, you had better be able to tell your Aggies from your Longhorns.

First let's get the school colors straight—orange and white/UT and maroon and white/A&M. At one point Texas considered orange and maroon, which would have confused matters, not to mention that this combination is illegal outside of Eastern Europe. The exact shade of orange was originally "burnt orange" but during WW II was changed to bright orange due to dye shortages. In 1967 the UT was back to its true colors. My Aggie friend says it took them that long to figure out the war was over.

UT's mascot is Bevo, the longhorn steer, of which there have been many. In 1915 the first steer was branded by some Aggies with the score of their win, 13-0. Ingenious UT students completed the brand so that it read "Bevo," which was the name of a "near beer." That mascot was so ill behaved that at the end of the year they served him up for a steak barbecue and invited the branding Aggies. Many other steers have followed in those famous hoof steps, and several have been "borrowed" by the Aggies.

The beautifully groomed, well-trained American Collie dog that proudly serves as mascot for A&M comes from a long line of collies, but the first "Reveille" was a mutt. Coming home from a game with Rice University in Houston, two Aggies hit a little black and white dog with their Model T. They put her in the car and carried her to the dorm, planning to take her to the vet the following morning. As dawn arrived and the bugler sounded reveille, she started barking and was christened "Reveille" on the spot. She took to marching with the band as she led them on and off the field. When she passed on to football heaven, she was buried at the north gate of Kyle Field, her head pointing toward the scoreboard so she would always know the score.

Once when UT students dognapped a very young Reveille VI, little Haley Duggen of Sugar Land wrote, begging, "Please take good care of Reveille. We love her very much." She signed her letter, "Future Aggie, class of 2008."

You will see Texas fans waving their hands with fingers contorted to form a steer head. One might think that this was discovered in those happy, lost 1960s when many of us played shadow puppets, but actually it was created on purpose. In 1955 head cheerleader Harley Clark Jr. wanted to have something special for the pep rally. He extended his forefinger and pinkie while holding the two middle fingers with his thumb and added the yell, "Hook 'em Horns!" At the game the next day, he was stunned when everyone was using the new hand signal and yell.

If you plan to join the students at an Aggie game, get a clean bill of health from your doctor and prior aerobics classes are recommended. The student body, known as "the twelfth man," stands throughout the game. That might be enough physical challenge, but no. They cross legs, link arms, and sway during the "Aggie War Hymn" and bend over—referred to as humping it—at the start of every yell. Aggies do yells, not cheers—led by yell leaders, not cheerleaders. Although it seems that the students are receiving ESP messages since they all know what the next yell will be, the yell leaders actually cue them with hand signals. They answer the "Hook 'em Horns" sign with a thumbs up, "Gig 'em Aggies."

Now, there are lots more great Texas college football teams, like the Texas Tech Red Raiders, the Texas Christian University Horned Frogs, the Baylor Bears, Southern Methodist University Mustangs, Rice University Owls, and the University of Houston Cougars, and we love them all. We may fight among ourselves about who's got the best team, but when a Texas team goes out of state we are all rooting for them.

We also have a professional football team that is known as "America's Team" at least around the Dallas area. But that would be a whole 'nother book.

Not to Brag But Heck, Why Not?

≥ ★ ≤

If there's a sport that has a championship, we have probably won it or are fixin' to. In the take-no-prisoners world of Texas sports, winning isn't the most important thing, it's the *only* thing. Pick a sport, any sport. That's a challenge! How about one that isn't indigenous to Texas, like say—hockey? Most of us didn't grow up on ice skates, but the Dallas Stars hockey team brought home the Stanley Cup Championship.

In the land of football we of course have many Heisman Trophy winners: Ricky Williams—Texas, Andre Ware—Houston, Earl Campbell—Texas, John David Crow—A&M, Doak Walker—SMU, and Davey O'Brien —TCU. In the world of round ball the San Antonio Spurs reign as NBA Champions. Women, too, as the Houston Comets have dominated the WNBA.

How about soccer? The U.S. Women's World Cup team champions included two women who were the products of Texas high school programs, and The Burn is more than just a passel of hunks. In baseball we have division leading teams—the Texas Rangers and the Houston Astros. And maybe you've heard of Hall of Famer Nolan Ryan? How about a World Series connected by I-45 with Nolan throwing out the first pitch?

The extraordinary Texas athlete, Lance Armstrong, stunned cycling fans around the world and inspired cancer survivors everywhere when he won the Tour de France title in 1999 after beating testicular cancer.

A lot of us did grow up playing tennis and golf, so we win big in those. Pro bowling, pro wrestling, cycling, track, or boxing—Texans excel. And we now have the outstanding Texas Motor Speedway and the beautiful Lone Star Park, so whether you enjoy fast cars or fast horses, we got 'em. Like I said, not to brag, but why not?

The One Sport We Don't Take Seriously: Politics

⋛ ★ ⋚

As with other popular sporting events, entertainment is a large part of the political scene in Texas. "Politics is show biz for ugly people," commented Bill Miller, a political consultant. With issues more convoluted than Ann Landers, many more laughs than the comics, about as much sound vision for the future as the astrology forecast, I relish the opinion page each morning. The vitriolic diatribes from the right and the left remind me of all I have missed in the years I was not privy to Texas state politics.

The first thing you may notice is that the typical party labels mean very little here. It is a sport, and therefore winning is the name of the game. Some folks have changed parties like other folks change their underwear. When former governor Connally switched parties to head Nixon's campaign, Liz Carpenter said, "It's a good thing John Connally wasn't at the Alamo. He'd be organizing the Texans for Santa Anna." Others stay in one party but consistently vote with the other party. Some are Democrats because their parents and grandparents were Democrats, so they honor the family tradition. I left Texas a primarily Democratic state, and Lyndon Baines Johnson was in the White House. When I returned there were Republicans everywhere, including the governor's mansion, perhaps headed for the White House. But I've noticed the rules of the game haven't changed—it's all about racking up yards for the score, scores for the win, and wins for the title.

Johnson envisioned a "Great Society" and was a consummate master at getting legislation passed using every Texas trick in the persuasive handbook, including horse trading. He said, "A long time ago I learned that telling a man to go to hell and making him go are two different propositions."

Although there was no love lost between him and Robert Kennedy, they managed to work together for civil rights. Bill Moyers, a journalist who knew Johnson well, said, "He was many things: proud, sensitive, impulsive, flamboyant, sentimental, earthy, mean at times, bold, euphoric, insecure, magnanimous, and the best dancer in the White House since Washington, but temperamental, melancholy, and strangely ill at ease, as well. He had an animal sense of weakness in other men, on whom he could inflict a hundred cuts." He was also very funny!

The Vietnam War loomed large over the Johnson administration. Once Senator Frank Church commented to the president that Walter Lippmann had some very good ideas on getting out of Vietnam. Johnson responded, "Next time you need a dam in Idaho, you just go ask Walter Lippmann." His former press secretary George Reedy said, "He may have been a son of a bitch, but he was a colossal son of a bitch."

Lyndon Johnson was not afraid to zig to the left or zag to the right in order to get into the end zone for the score. His former assistant L. E. Jones said, "Winning is the name of the game. I have no doubt that he could have become either an ultra-liberal or ultra-conservative, if that would have brought victory." And Lyndon could charm the reason out of folks. He reveled in his own influence saying, "I'm a powerful S.O.B, you know that?"

Lyndon had an incredible mentor in Sam Rayburn. Sam was a Texan and Speaker of the U.S. House of Representatives for a longer stint than anybody else in history. Sam was the consummate politician who said, "I like power, and I like to use it." From the beginning of his career he clearly understood what the game was all about and knew how to disarm a constituency. "I will not deny that there are men in the district better qualified than I to go to Congress, but gentlemen, these men are not in the race." Always cutting to the quick, he said, "Politics is the art of the impossible." He also recognized the practical mechanics of the political game. "A congressman's first duty is to get re-elected."

Winning elections in Texas is certainly what it's all about, whether we're talking the local school board, city council, House or Senate, or high school cheerleader. Yeah, you probably heard about the Texas mom who was so determined that her daughter be elected cheerleader, she hired a hit man to kill an opponent's mother. As she poured out her desire to an undercover cop, she said, "The things you do for your kids."

Then there was the Representative who hired his cousin to shoot him, just wing him really, so he could claim that his enemies had attacked him. He blamed the satanic and communistic cult that was against his strong stand for the American way. When the "crime" was solved, the law went looking for him and found him hiding at his mother's house, in a stereo cabinet. The ever glib Molly Ivins quipped, "He always did want to be speaker."

Miriam "Ma" Ferguson won the governorship after her husband, James "Pa" Ferguson, was impeached and removed from office. She didn't care for the idea of teaching foreign languages in public schools. She said, "If the English language was good enough for Jesus Christ, it is good enough for the children of Texas." Molly Ivins said, "On growing up female in Texas; I had a choice of role models—Ma Ferguson or the Kilgore Rangerettes."

Former governor Ann Richards brought a sound wit to the office. She said, "I feel very fortunate, truthfully, that there was a treatment program for my disease [alcoholism]. I wish there were a treatment program for meanness, and then maybe Jim Mattox [her opponent] could get well." Humorist Cactus Pryor said, "Ann Richards would save the state $5,000 a year if she'd give up Spray Net." In an address to the Smith College graduating class, Richards said, "Back when dinosaurs roamed the earth, and I was your age, politics was a male province. Women made the coffee, and men made the decisions." At the 1988 Democratic National Convention, Richards said of Bush, "Poor George. He can't help it. He was born with a silver foot in his mouth."

Bush has always had a way with words. "Read my lips" and "No new taxes" springs to mind. Some folks don't count the senior Bush as a Texan, but I remember my mother dragging me across the floor at the Houston River Oaks Country Club to meet "The man who will be president one day."

Quoting Bush was always a challenge for the press. "So we got home last night—I say 'home'—we did. Climbed into bed. And I—nervous guy, you know, tension and work—my system working on the 6 a.m. call." And he always told us a little more than we needed to know, like the personal life of Millie, the White House dog. "This happened yesterday, a beautiful experience. We expect to have puppies in the White House." When explaining why he chose to sit in the stands instead of the private suite at the baseball park in Arlington, he said, "I want the folks to see me sitting in the same seat they sit in, eating the same popcorn, peeing in the same urinal." See what I mean, more than we needed to know.

The junior George W. proves that the berry doesn't fall far from the Bush. He was quoted as saying, "After six years, or five years, or actually four and one half years, to get it correct—four and a half years of having been, actually four years and five months, of having been in [the governor's] office, my enthusiasm and optimism about life has not waned." But the reporters were pooped!

No one could surpass in eloquence the former Texas Speaker of the House Gib Lewis. Here is a man who created state-of-the-art double-speak and politico-babble. Upon his re-election as Speaker, he was deeply moved and declared, "I am filled with humidity." While suggesting that state employee numbers could be reduced in a more natural way, he said, "We should not fire people, but accomplish it through employee nutrition." Don't know what he was going to add to their diets. Molly Ivins observed that, "A teacher publicly challenged Gib Lewis' consistently bad syntax. "What sin tax? I'm not for any sin tax. I'm against all new taxes," Gib ad-libbed.

Waggoner Carr, former Texas attorney general, is a great storyteller and shares lots of good ones in his book aptly titled *Texas Politics in My Rearview Mirror*. He had a good friendship with fellow Texan Lyndon Johnson, who gave him some advice early in his career: "#1 Never pass up a free meal, and #2 Never pass up an opportunity to go to the men's room!" Johnson also complained to Waggoner in a visit at the LBJ ranch about his lack of freedom as president.

"You know, Waggoner, ever since I was a young boy, the very last thing I did every night before going to bed was go outside and relieve myself while looking up at the moon and millions of stars. As I stood there beholding that wondrous sight in complete privacy, I understood the true meaning of freedom. The first time I tried doing that out here after I became president, a Secret Service car spotlight was on me immediately, and you know how painful it is to try to stop the flow once you're started. They know better than that now, but I don't have the freedom to do that at the White House, and I miss it."

When Ross Perot burst onto the presidential campaign trail with a rapid-fire delivery in a voice like fingernails on a blackboard and a chart to explain everything, the nation took notice. Texans had been aware of the Dallas billionaire for years. Ivins labeled him, "an unguided missile," and said he was, "a man with a mind a half-inch wide." But no one could have written him better material than he came up with on his own. "If anybody has any better ideas, I'm all ears."

He felt called to the race even though, "Jeez, I've never run for dogcatcher." His supporters twisted his arm, while he "ah, shucked," determining that, "We certainly don't have the most able people in our society running for president. We are getting people who will endure anything because of their power drive." George W. said to his father, "We could be in trouble," when he saw a kid selling a bunch of "Ross Perot for President" T-shirts.

Campaigning, Perot said, "I can't tell you how many times somebody told me, 'You're the best qualified candidate. It's a shame you're not going to win.' I'd tell them, 'If everyone who felt that way would vote for me, I might win'." The always glib Gib Lewis said, "Perot is a man who has extinguished himself in many fields." He certainly made a bid in politics, racking up an amazing twenty percent of the vote in the '92 election. "I want to shock the system so that people will talk issues." We were shocked—no doubt.

When George W. decided to aim for the governor's mansion, about all we knew about him was that he was a part-owner of the Texas Rangers and his daddy had been president. He was quick to parlay the baseball card, if you will. "The reason people can relate to baseball is that it's the sport that normal-sized people can play." He presented himself as a real Texan, good ol' boy, distinguishing himself from his dad. "He attended Greenwich Country Day, and I went to San Jacinto High School in Midland, Texas." He also liked to open his speeches with, "I know that you would have liked to have the most famous Bush here tonight, but my mother was busy." He was pretty confident about Texas voters, "They'll like me, too, if they just get a whiff of me." Dubya, as we call him, wants us to know he's a Texan.

There's an old story in Texas about a young man running for office who was going door to door to get the feel for what the average voter thought. He asked one elderly gentleman if he agreed that ignorance and apathy were the real problems in our democracy. The old man didn't skip a beat and responded, "I don't know, and I don't care!"

On the Eighth Day God Created Texas

≥ ☆ ≤

In the introduction, when I explained that religion was political, you may have been confused. Let me explain by example. Of course, there are many different brands of worship in Texas, and most folks belong to one or another. We tend to be very loyal to whatever one we choose, but we don't talk about it much. We don't want to offend anyone. We believe that's politically correct, right? You might know Jim Bob for forty years and know everything about him, like how he takes his coffee, how he votes, and where his deer lease is and such, except not know his religion of choice. Since we don't talk about it much, we have to be very careful at all times about what we say, so as not to offend. This can call for some fancy steppin' as when tellin' jokes and such. Folks will carefully check out the room before launching into a story about the preacher who went into a bar. Be very careful.

Whatever your choice is, a place of worship is a great way to meet folks when you move to a new community. Just remember at most places you need to wait to be seated so you don't mistakenly sit in the pew where the Jones family has been sitting since they donated all the stained glass windows, back in ought two. You will also notice that although most Sunday services are an hour in length, some are only fifty minutes. This is in order to give their folks a head start for the restaurants. Honest. I have a girlfriend who is not a churchgoer, a lovely woman, but not a churchgoer. She goes to Wal-Mart on Sunday morning and enjoys her shopping, but she does get all dressed up in case she runs late and sees someone she knows.

We all know that children will say the darndest things—out of the mouths of babes, and all that. My mother loves to tell about the day she was teaching a Sunday school class of four-year-olds. Her lesson was based on the scripture "God is Love." She was trying to quiet them down as they were walking around the table chanting, "God is Love, God is Love," round and round the table. Mom quietly said, "I want you to sit down now and close your eyes and listen carefully." As soon as they were seated with eyes squeezed shut she read, "Be still and know that I am God." It worked quite well and the lesson was a success. The following Sunday when the children were seated, Mom asked, "Now, who can remember from last week, who is God?" In unison, the children chirped, "YOU ARE!"

Another time Mom was teaching about all the blessings we receive. "All good gifts come from God," she said. A little tyke piped up, "Then what does Santa do?"

Geri Ann tells about the time they were building a new church. In order to raise money, folks were asked to donate one thousand dollars for a pew and to choose three hymns for the hymnal. Her grandmother, Gertie, pointed at some handsome young men and said, "I choose him and him and him!"

Holidaze

> ★ <

Nobody loves holidays as much as Texans. Now in most places I've lived folks have gotten into some pretty serious decorations at Christmastime, but for Texans that's just the apex of the calendar of special events that all require elaborate decoration collections.

All doors including garage doors, yards, roofs, fences, and vehicles are festooned for Valentine's Day, St. Patrick's Day, Easter, Cinco de Mayo, the Fourth of July, Octoberfest, and of course the holiday season that begins the day after All Hollows Eve. Ghosts and goblins make way for Santas, snowmen, and reindeer that stay up until Super Bowl Sunday. And you've got your Stars and Stripes that must be displayed on all the national holidays.

Humble little trailers and cottages that might be passed unnoticed suddenly explode with chili pepper lights, Santa's legs sticking out of a fake chimney, Rudolf sitting spraddle-legged on the roof with a Budwieser, and a tractor wrapped in twinkle lights that make the wheels look like they're spinning. Entire lawns, all tree trunks, bushes, and roofs that are embellished as brightly as downtown Las Vegas at night look like impending electrical disasters of tangled extension cords in the blaze of daylight. Valentines Day folks have huge hearts with "I love you, Vickie Sue" spelled out in potted red zinnias. Everything and everybody is totally green for at least two weeks in March. Just check out Dublin and Shamrock, Texas!

Around Easter there are front yards with six-foot-tall bunny dummies posed in lawn chairs and pastel colored plastic Easter eggs adorning bushes and trees. And Halloween houses are draped in webs, leaves are gathered in huge jack-o-lantern trash bags, and hundreds of friendly ghosts hang in the spooky webbed trees. The thing that blows my mind is that all of these people have all of these seasonal decorations and have the time to put them up! Don't these folks have jobs? I'm just jealous 'cause I still have unmailed holiday cards from 1987.

The Texas Music Mosaic

☆

John Lennon, Maria Callas, and Elvis were not Texans, but every other musician of any consequence was! Too strong a statement you say? A gross exaggeration maybe? Well, I might have stretched the blanket a bit, but it's not as big a whopper as you might think. A very good case can be made that Texas has produced more significant musical performers than any other place. The mind-blowing thing to me is the wide variety of musical styles and traditions represented by celebrated Texan talents. The lists are staggering with the likes of Janis Joplin, George Jones, Van Cliburn, Boz Scaggs, Bob Wills, Selena, Delbert McClinton, Roy Orbison, Lyle Lovett, Mark Chestnutt, ZZ Top, Edie Brickell, Hagfish, Tanya Tucker, Buddy Holly, Al Escovedo, Blind Lemon Jefferson, Gene Autry, Willie Nelson, Scott Joplin, Roger Miller, Barry White—impressed yet? The list goes on and on.

Texans in Country

≳ ⭐ ≲

Long before "singing cowboys" made it big in the movies, Texas cowboys sang. Long cattle drives up the Chisholm Trail cultivated story telling, cowboy poetry, and songs around the campfire after a long hard day. And then Will Rogers bumped into a little guy from Texas who was working at a telegraph station in Oklahoma. Encouraged by Rogers, the young man from Tioga took to his guitar and became the incredible cowboy singing sensation Gene Autry. Mr. Autry was always my mother's favorite, and "The Yellow Rose of Texas," "Tumbling Tumbleweeds," "Back in the Saddle Again," along with the first song I learned all the words to, "You Are My Sunshine," were all major hits for Autry. And I don't know what kids would do at holidays without "Rudolph the Red Nosed Reindeer," "Here Comes Santa Claus," and "Here Comes Peter Cottontail." Autry starred in movies and traveled the country establishing the glory of the West in the hearts of his fans. My mother fell in love with him at the rodeos in Dublin, Texas.

Tex Ritter, intelligently shunning his first name of Maurice, studied the cowboy life with the likes of J. Frank Dobie at the University of Texas and then started his singing career on the radio at Houston's KPRC. Some of his hits included "Boll Weevil," "Blood on the Saddle," and "Deck of Cards." He also captured a coveted Academy Award for the unforgettable theme of "High Noon."

Autry and Ritter set the stage for the western part of what came to be known as "country & western" music. "The Father of Country Music" was a railroad brakeman from Mississippi by the name of Jimmy Rogers. The man who dazzled audiences with his yodel, suffering from ill health, moved to Kerrville and then to San Antonio. This generous man worked right up to the end, giving benefit performances for flood victims and completing his last song, "Fifteen Years Ago Today," just before he died.

After the repeal of Prohibition, honky-tonks sprang up all around Texas. Fiddle-driven dance bands were experimenting with infusing the blues with Tex-Mex, Cajun, and German polka sounds. Bob Wills left his barbering in Turkey, Texas, and formed the Texas Playboys. Texas swing was on its way with hits like "San Antonio Rose." Another popular group was founded by Milton Brown from Stephenville, Texas, called the Musical Brownies. They were the most popular band around until his death in a car wreck in 1936. Brown and Wills played together as the Wills Fiddle Band and later became the Light Crust Doughboys. The Doughboys are still playing and have spawned many great country musicians.

When the likes of Ernest Tubb, Ray Price, and Lefty Frizzell came along, honky-tonk music took hold and paved the way for Buck Owens from Sherman, Texas, and Jim Reeves from Galloway, Texas. Texas was feeding Nashville's Grand Ole Opry some fine fodder, but we couldn't have been ready for the Ol' Possum and the Red Headed Stranger.

Since the day George Jones was born in Saratoga, reportedly shouting, "The Race Is On," he has been in a death grip with life. He has lived out practically every country song ever written—boozin' and loosin' and yet managing to contribute authentic country classics like, "If My Heart Had Windows" and "Walk Through This World With Me." He married the incredible Tammy

Wynette, but his drinking didn't slow down as he became known for no-shows. Although their relationship ended, who can keep a dry eye when we hear "He Stopped Loving Her Today." After a near fatal car crash, Jones is back on his feet, and we hope for more proof of his incredible talent in the future.

Willie Nelson, born in Abbott, has led the outlaw move that has established Austin as a musical mecca. His career started as he sold vacuums and encyclopedias by day and wrote and played in clubs by night. His songs began to sell, and with "The Party's Over" he became known as a singer/songwriter. Nelson, who never quite fit in with the rhinestone and fringe crowd of Nashville, came home to Texas reborn as a beacon for progressive country/rock types across the nation. And they came!

Bill Arhos at KLRU (PBS affiliate), producer Paul Bosner, and director David Scafe cooked up the idea to feature the music boom that was heating up in Austin in the early seventies. The result of their brainstorm was and still is *Austin City Limits*. They sold the PBS bosses on the idea with a pilot starring none other than Willie Nelson and got themselves underwritten for the series' first thirteen episodes. In 1976 the first show aired, featuring Asleep at the Wheel and a reunited Original Texas Playboys from the old Bob Wills' Western Swing band. The show has featured many national artists but has always celebrated Texas bred talents like Lyle Lovett, Stevie Ray Vaughan, the Fabulous Thunderbirds, and more recently Fastball and Shawn Colvin. Colvin told *Good Morning America*, "Austin is just a great music town." Ain't that the truth. If you get the chance, try to get into the audience for a taping. To find out about tickets you can call the ACL hotline (512-475-9077).

Waylon Jennings was born in Littlefield and got to know Buddy Holly. When he moved to Lubbock, he quickly became a Cricket. Jennings would have been on that fateful small plane flight had he not let J. P. "The Big Bopper" Richardson have his seat. He also fought the Nashville establishment and joined with Nelson, Jerry Jeff Walker ("Mr. Bojangles"), Guy Clark ("L. A. Freeway" and "Desperados"), Michael Murphy, Gary P. Nunn, Michael Martin Murphey—and their numbers grew.

Jerry Jeff Walker is one of the famous Mad Dogs (literati and musicians like Nelson, Larry King of "Best Little Whorehouse in Texas" fame, Gary Cartwright, Bud Shark, and Jay Milliner) who so influenced Texas culture in the sixties and seventies and almost killed themselves being creative and having too much fun. Jerry Jeff has a voice that could peel paint off a barn, but he sure does grow on you.

Standing just apart from this talented crowd was the terminally offensive and delightful Kinky Friedman with his band, the Texas Jewboys. Some of his hits included "They Aren't Makin' Jews Like Jesus Anymore" and "Get Your Biscuits in the Oven and Your Buns in the Bed." He also writes pseudo-mystery novels that make folks laugh out loud.

The seventies brought us Kenny Rogers, who could smoothly cover just about any ol' tune and it would sell; the wil'chil', Tanya Tucker from Seminole; Floydada's own Don Williams ("I Believe in You"); Barbara Mandrell from Houston; Larry Gatlin and the Gatlin Brothers; Janie Fricke (who moved to a ranch outside of Dallas); and Johnny Lee, who was born in Texas City ("Looking for Love").

George Strait, born in Pearsal, ushered in "young country" along with other artists who revered the work of Bob Wills and the integrity of "Pure Country" roots. He was joined by Radney Foster, Holly Dunn, Clint Black, Ronnie Dunn (of Brooks and Dunn fame), Hal Ketchum, Tracy Lawrence, Lee Roy Parnell, Mark Chesnutt, Tracy Byrd, and Clay Walker.

Lyle Lovett stands alone as the man who can turn a thought-provoking lyric to a belly laugh probably faster than any other writer. The tall lanky, hair-challenged Texan has much to offer, especially in a concert venue where you will discover why Julia Roberts was smitten with him. You will be, too.

There's a new wave forming, and many believe Texas singer/songwriters are at the crest of it. Clubs are booking the likes of Robert Earl Keen. Keen is a Houston boy, a Texas A&M graduate (like Lyle Lovett) who actually hung out with Lovett and Bryan Duckworth. He sings about the funny-sad life that is lived by outsiders in small-town bars on Saturday nights. When I asked the owners of City Limits in Stephenville who their favorite act was, V. W. and Cynthia Stevens said in unison, "Robert Earl Keen." He has had a big cult following for some time now but is destined for a wider audience, and we are all lucky for that.

The beautiful blond Dixie Chicks are burning up the charts and winning awards right and left. They have Grammies, Country Music Awards, and Academy of Country Music Awards. "Chicks Rule" is becoming quite the catch phrase for young girls who want to imitate them, and that's a good thing because they have an honesty that success hasn't ruined.

Alternative country is gaining momentum and moving into larger venues with groups like Ruthie and the Wranglers, Hot Club of Cowtown, and Dale Watson—honky-tonker extraordinare. Folks want to hear something fresh and different from the slick Nashville hat acts, and Texas clubs are responding.

If you have a hankering to be a star yourself, head up north to the Panhandle and sign up at South Plains College in Loveland. This school offers an Associate of Arts degree from the Creative Arts Department, which has amazing programs where you can learn to be a sound tech or a performer in bluegrass, country, rock, R&B, tejano, or contemporary Christian music! Your instructors will be seasoned performers who like to help new talent get a start. The likes of Lee Ann Womack, the Dixie Chicks' own Gnarly Amines, Scott Summer of the Tom T. Hall, and many others. October through May they even have a show on campus called "Thursday Nite Live."

God bless Texas country music!

Texas Rock

⋛ ★ ⋚

Charles Hardin Holley, a high school student in Lubbock, formed a band he called the Western and Bop Band. Never heard of Charles? Well, he became Buddy Holly. After he added the Crickets to his band, his rock take on "That'll Be the Day" became one of his tunes that would set the music scene on its ear. All of us who were teens at the time remember how a geek with a guitar became a sex symbol and then an icon upon his tragic death. The movie *The Buddy Holly Story* still makes us cry.

Roy Orbison and the Teen Kings were part of the rock scene in the fifties, and he went on to have a long career with hits like "Only the Lonely," "Blue Angel," "Crying," and "Pretty Woman." Joined by the surviving Crickets, Sam the Sham and the Pharaohs, ? and the Mysterians, Mouse and the Traps, and Dallas's Trini Lopez ("Lemon Tree"), Bobby Fuller ("I Fought the Law"), Roy Head ("Treat Her Right"), The Five Americans from Dallas, Texas rocked. Houston's Kenny Rogers jumped from the New Christie Minstrels and formed Kenny Rogers and the First Edition.

You might not know that Stephen Stills was from Dallas. He hooked up with David Crosby and Graham Nash to form a little group you probably have heard of—Crosby, Stills and Nash. The group expanded to include Neil Young and churned out many hits.

"The Monkees," made-for-TV show and group, brought to the fore a crazed genius by the name of Michael Nesmith. My maiden name was Nesmith and so my sister and I always claimed to be Michael's cousins.

We carried on that fraud for years. You know his mom invented "white out," without which I would have never made it through grad school. He would go on to produce a masterpiece of video called "Elephant Parts," then on to feature films and many other brilliant ventures.

Don Henley is from Gilmer, Texas, and helped to form the Eagles. Steve Miller (Steve Miller Blues Band) and Boz Scaggs and Sylvester "Sly" Stone (Sly and the Family Stone) were all from Dallas. The move in the late sixties was to the San Francisco Bay area.

But the full throttle, whiskey laced belter who would tear our hearts out with her soulful renditions of "Try (Just a Little Bit Harder)," "Kozmic Blues," and the Kris Kristofferson penned "Me and Bobby McGee" was Janis Joplin. She was writing plays in the first grade in Port Arthur. Her school days weren't happy ones, and she started drinking and hanging with a bad crowd. Yet she made good grades and went on to the University of Texas, where she was nominated for the "Ugliest Man on Campus" contest. No wonder she fled for Haight-Ashbury and heroin.

When she died, she was working on a new song entitled "I Just Made Love to 25,000 People But I'm Going Home Alone." She was only twenty-seven when she died of an overdose. *The Rose* is a film starring Bette Midler that, although fiction, tells a lot of the truth about this haunted talent. I recently purchased *Box of Pearls: The Janis Joplin Collection* and her passionate rhythm and vocal perfection shines.

Kris Kristofferson is famous for his classic song "Help Me Make It Through the Night" and his acting in many movies. He is a native of Brownsville and was a Rhodes scholar.

ZZ Top blasted on the scene more than twenty years ago and continues to rock us today. They chose the "ZZ" after Texas bluesman Z. Z. Hill. The "Top" came from a remark about the old Z-shaped beams on the hayloft doors. A friend of Billy Gibbons said, "Look, ZZ Top," and the band was branded. Billy went to high school in Houston with my sister and played with a band called the Royal Coachmen. He called her "Fireball," and if you know Cathy, you know that's appropriate. She remembers him being a great guy who organized a "peaceful" demonstration where the students just dropped their books and walked out. "We didn't really make it out the door—we felt we had made our point," she remembers. Those were the radical days.

Johnny and Edgar Winter, Edie Brikell (New Bohemians, "What I Am"), and the incomparable Jimmy Vaughan and Stevie Ray Vaughan all have joined the Texas sounds that make the state an amazing force in the music world. In the Lone Star State the beat goes on—and on!

Most of us got to know our favorite artists listening to them on the radio. Radio pioneer Gordon McClendon helped create the Top-40 format and founded the ever-popular KLIF in Dallas. He promoted his DJs and thought up unbelievable publicity stunts to get folks to remember the station's call letters. One time he tossed balloons filled with money out of the window of a downtown hotel, which snarled up rush-hour traffic. He also came up with the idea for all-news and easy-listening formats. He was the first station owner to have a mobile news unit on the scene of breaking stories. He passed away in 1986 and was later inducted into the Radio Hall of Fame.

Tejano

≳ ✭ ≲

Tejano music takes its name from Tejanos, which is what Texans are called in Mexico. This is a seductive Latin sound that blends pop, rock, and Mexican influences with Caribbean dance music. It has caught fire with the likes of Selena, Ricky Martin, and Mark Anthony. Texas artists include La Mafia, Laura Canales, Emilio Navaira, David Lee Garza, Grupo Mazz, and, of course, the exciting Selena who died too soon.

Selena Quintannilla Perez was born in Lake Jackson and won a 1994 Grammy for Best Mexican-American Album with *Selena Live!* Proclaimed the "queen of tejano music" she was gunned down in Corpus Christi. Her influence continues with a successful movie of her life and many young female artists who honor her music. Her husband is coming out with an album, and she will not soon be forgotten.

A group that has performed for more than thirty years is showcased in Temple at the Little Joe Museum. The group known as Little Joe y Familia is featured along with the Ramon Hernandez Hispanic Entertainment Archives.

Urban Cowboys

⫶ ★ ⫶

Texas is a beautiful combination of rural landscapes, small towns, suburbs, and strong, beautiful cities where skyscrapers glisten and the urban energy calls us to work and play. Our cities have personalities as distinct as each of our small towns, but no matter which one you are in, you still know you are in Texas. If you are moving to one of our cities, get to know your new home by contacting the local chamber of commerce. These folks will send you a relocation packet with info on jobs, schools, churches, arts centers, and entertainment. Check out the web for information through your favorite search engine. Get to know your local newspaper by subscribing for delivery and even on-line. This will give you a great feel for local politics, business, the arts, and sports. Also get travel information because you will want to check out all of the sights around your new stomping grounds.

Friends you had forgotten that you ever had will want to come and visit you in Texas, and you will enjoy showing off your city with its clean, vibrant downtown. Just as small towns throughout Texas have been revitalized, so have our cities been refurbished with great vision for the future. You will want to visit all of our cities, and each trip will be a distinct and unique experience.

Music, Learnin', and Politics Right Here in River City

≷ ★ ≶

If you think you are planning to just make a visit to Austin, Texas, be careful. Many of the locals you will meet thought the same thing. They dropped into town to catch some cool tunes on Sixth Street and years later found themselves dressed in Berkenstocks and five-pocket khaki shorts with two or three advanced degrees. They are waiting tables at an upscale eatery at night and spending days volunteering as environmentalist activists and jamming after hours with a blues band.

Now if you are really planning to move to Austin on purpose, I presume that you have a law degree. This is a requirement for claiming residency since you are also probably planning to run for public office. Lyndon Johnson said, "Many Texas towns are too small to support one lawyer, but none are too small to support two lawyers." Austin is big enough to support ninety-three pages of lawyers as evidenced in the Yellow Pages. Some are full-paged ads, of course, and a couple include photos that suspiciously look like the casts from popular TV lawyer shows.

The first thing that overwhelms you is the outright beauty of the place. Downtown is a combination of skyscrapers and history, as this is the capital of Texas. If you were expecting dusty plains, you will be amazed by the gorgeous views of lakes, tree-covered hills, rolling farmlands, and colorful vegetation everywhere.

The Texas Colorado River runs right through downtown as it winds its way to the Gulf of Mexico. Beautiful

Lake Travis bends and stretches across the western edge of the city, and Lake Austin and Town Lake cross the downtown area. These lakes were formed by a series of dams, which were built to control flooding and provide recreation almost year round. One of the city's nicknames is "River City."

The city was founded on the site of a small community of four families known as Waterloo. Five scouts were looking for a proper location for the new capital city for the Republic of Texas. It was then named in honor of the "Father of Texas," Stephen F. Austin.

Austin is one of the most highly educated communities in the United States, and these folks read a lot of books—racking up the highest bookstore sales in the country at $195 per household. The opportunities for higher learning are vast, including: Austin Community College, Austin Presbyterian Theological Seminary, Concordia Lutheran College, Episcopal Theological Seminary of the Southwest, Huston-Tillotson College, St. Edwards University, and the University of Texas at Austin.

The title of "Live Music Capital of the World" is well deserved as any weekend visit to the Sixth Street area will confirm. Walking from club to club with the swarms of people of all ages, you will experience the sounds of talented groups on their way to stardom and seasoned veterans who just enjoy the reality of a small room and an appreciative crowd. You may be surprised at the diversity of musical styles offered in the Victorian and native-stone buildings that populate this historic street, once known as Old Pecan Street. The restoration of this area, basically seven blocks between I-35 and Congress Avenue, has brought restaurants, clubs, specialty shops, and art galleries to what was once Austin's main street.

Whatever your musical bent, Austin has it: the blues, country/western, tejano, reggae, jazz, conjunto, swing, and rock. Public Broadcasting Stations put the eyes of the nation on the local music scene with its long-running hit series *Austin City Limits*. After living in several parts of the country, popular performer Shawn Colvin decided to join many other artists, native Texans, and born-agains, who have settled their families in Austin.

The movie industry is also booming in Texas with Austin becoming a mecca for film production. Successful Texans have forsaken Hollywood and returned to their home state to be born again. Independent studios are blossoming, and the amazing variety of terrain makes the state a movie location scout's dream.

Austin is the Southwest's center for high tech computer industries, encouraging the nickname "Silicon Hills." So if lawyering, the music business, movie stardom, continuous education, or politics don't appeal to you, remember that the Dell phenomenon was hatched right over there on the University of Texas campus. Michael got bored with school since he was making so much money, and Houston's Compaq executives are losing sleep trying to figure out what happened.

The **Capitol** complex is well worth a visit. It is comprised of the magnificent classic state house made of beautiful natural pink Texas granite and the surrounding, carefully groomed forty-six acres of parklands. A guided tour will give your family an appreciation for the restoration and renovation project that restored the Capitol building to its former splendor.

A couple of must-sees involve the LBJ legacy. The **Lyndon Baines Johnson Library and Museum** includes exhibits featuring everything from campaign memorabilia to a moon rock and a replica of the Oval Office. The **National Wildflower Research Center**, which was founded by Lady Bird Johnson, includes forty-two acres of gardens, landscaped areas, and themed display gardens. The center also serves as an educational organization with classes and workshops highlighting beautification and conservation.

Checking out the music scene is a must-do, so here are some great suggestions in several popular categories. For blues, the "you must hear it to believe it" place is **Antone's**, 213 W. 5th Street, where the blues were officially rebirthed. If it is country your heart desires, two-step over to the **Broken Spoke**, 3201 S. Lamar, where families all dance together to western swing and progressive country in this authentic honky-tonk. On the UT campus, 24th and Guadalupe, check out the **Cactus Cafe**, which books top-flight acoustic acts nightly. The best of tejano music (but no conjunto) is found at the **Club Carnaval**, 2237 E. Riverside Drive, along with popular music from Mexico. If you want conjunto, that hot Austin Tex-Mex dance music with the accordion driven polkas, head over to **El Pepe Polka**,1523 Tinnin Ford Road. Those will get you started, but you will find music treasures all around the town, "The Live Music Capital of the World!"

Now you are ready to spend a day on Sixth Street. You will discover that the east side is probably younger, trendier, and absolutely a carnival/zoo on the weekends while the west side is more sedate and upscale. Start out at the now famous **Whole Foods Market**, 601 N. Lamar, and enjoy the deli treats like Mexican empanadas, Greek dolmas, grilled eggplant, and elegant salads.

Right next door try to catch up with the locals in reading purchases at the **Book People**, 601 N. Lamar Blvd, where you can sink into a comfy armchair and sip a cup of joe as you make your selections. **Eclectic**, 700 N. Lamar Blvd, is an outlet offering goods from around the world. At 1009 W. 6th St. discover the treasures from seventy dealers at **Whit Hanks Antiques**. Continue your adventure and you will discover art galleries, designer fashions, and exotic imports beyond your wildest dreams. Yeah, you are really in Texas.

If you have time to linger in the Austin area, there are some incredibly unique and just plain lovely towns just a few miles out that deserve your attention. Go north on I-35 to **Round Rock**, named for the large rock in the bed of Brushy Creek; farther on enjoy the beautifully restored Victorian downtown of **Georgetown**; or jog down F.M. 1431 to **Lago Vista** to appreciate its breathtaking namesake, the lake view. Turn south and head to **Wimberly** where many artists make their home and on to **San Marcos** where Aquarena Springs offers cruises on the San Marcos River.

Megalopolis-Metropolis-Metroplex

⋛ ★ ⋚

In North Texas we refer to the area that includes Dallas, Fort Worth, Arlington, Irving, and surrounding communities as "The Metroplex." It covers more than one hundred square miles and is home to about four million folks. Many newbees, who had been transplanted from some urban giant on one of the non-Gulf coasts, believed that they were escaping to some cuddly little warm, fuzzy small town with a folksy name like Farmers Branch, Grand Prarie, North Richland Hills, or Carrollton. They were soon jolted to reality when they discovered themselves sitting in traffic, sucking up bus fumes—they had moved to "The Metroplex."

From the highways and loops it is easy to mistake this massive population center as simply chains of fast food restaurants that repeat in order—hamburger, fried chicken, tacos, and pizza—ad nauseum. Surely these communities couldn't have distinct personalities, could they? Is an armadillo in the road flat? Now any Texan will defend any other Texan from any outside attack, but just try to get a Dallasite to venture into Fort Worth or vicey vercy, and you will see some heels dig in deep. A Fort Worth resident who was asked by a Fort Worth, Texas magazine to imagine a move to Dallas, responded that he would rather stick a red-hot poker in his eye while parked on Stemmons Freeway, and then asked, " . . . Do I have to move to Dallas?"

Big D - Little a - Double L - A - S

If you don't have an allegiance such as the Fort Worth man, moving to Dallas can be a rich experience. "Rich" as in the Southwest's biggest banking center, insurance center, and wholesale business domain, ranking third in the nation in "million dollar" businesses and second in convention sites. My girlfriend Karen, a longtime resident of the city, says, "It has an electricity, an energy. It's so alive, and that just doesn't say it." But she does admit that the city's downtown area looks like it was "designed by a freshman architecture student. I mean we have this city hall that looks like it is gonna topple into the reflection pool, and what is it with those balls?" Obviously the locals got excited about the gold, giant glass icons long before they moved to other cites, but nobody imagined how difficult it would be to drive into the glare of the reflected sun. Oops!

This sophisticated city is a center of style and design. Be sure to bring your "glam" duds, or buy them here. There are more than thirty wholesale fashion and home furnishing markets each year in "Big D." The Dallas Market Center complex includes Home Furnishings Mart, INFOMART, World Trade Center, Trade Mart, Apparel Mart, Decorative Center District, and Menswear Mart. The city that started as a trading post is now the shopping champion of the Americas, with more shopping centers per capita than any other city in the U.S. As I said, "rich"—as in bring your credit cards.

In order to bone up on Dallas history, I highly recommend *The Unauthorized History of Dallas* by the incomparable Rose-Mary Rumbley. Dr. Rumbley has a way of teaching you in spite of your convolutions of laughter. I was in the audience once when she was talking about C.C. Slaughter, who was a generous benefactor of early Dallas. She told us when he pledged a bunch of money for a hospital, the directors, though much indebted to him, couldn't bear to name the facility "Slaughter Hospital."

Whether you are vacationing in or moving to the Dallas area, you should take advantage of the sights and sounds this cultural center has to offer. Forget what you think you learned from the nighttime soap *Dallas* or more recently, *Walker, Texas Ranger*; the real Dallas is a mecca for the arts and artists.

The Dallas Museum of Art boasts superb collections of pre-Columbian art and major European and American art, located in a lovely building in the **Dallas Arts District**. While in the area, visit the **Atrium Cafe** and the **Trammell Crow Center**, which has an indoor/outdoor sculpture plaza with pieces including Rodins. The **Dallas Symphony Orchestra**, consistently ranked in the nation's top ten, performs a full schedule in the **Morton H. Meyerson Symphony Hall**, a multimillion-dollar facility. Theatrical productions take place at the **Dallas Theatre Center** designed by Frank Lloyd Wright.

While partaking in the sophisticated sights and sounds, add taste, as in the tasteful epicurean experience of **The Mansion on Turtle Creek**, 2821 Turtle Creek Boulevard. Chef Dean Fearing, star of *Great Chefs* on the Food Channel, creates the epitome of upscale cuisine like lobster tacos. Surrounded by understated elegance, you will have a dining event to be remembered.

No trip would be complete without a tour of the **Deep Ellum Historic District**. This several block area, just east of downtown, is the home of shops, restaurants, and clubs featuring music from country to rock. But certainly home of the blues.

Another must-see is the **State Fair Park** where twenty-four attractions, including seven museums, will keep your family entertained. **The Science Place**—filled with more than two hundred and fifty hands-on exhibits, **Dallas Aquarium**—home to more than three hundred and seventy-five species of aquatic animals, and the **Museum of Natural History**—with a wide collection of native animal life in authentic habitat groups will all thrill curious kids of all ages. The **National Women's Museum** is scheduled to open in 2000.

The **Age of Steam Museum** offers a nostalgic look at the golden age of railroads, including the world's largest steam locomotive. The **Museum of African-American Life and Culture** documents just that. Also check out the **Cotton Bowl** that hosts the traditional Texas-Oklahoma game during State Fair, which is held in October. Find Fair Park on Robert Collum Blvd. at Grand.

If Oliver Stone hasn't convinced or confused you enough, a visit to the **Sixth Floor Museum** may confuse or convince you as to the event that is imprinted in the memories of those of us old enough to remember where we were when John F. Kennedy was assassinated.

Another nightmare from history is vividly documented, so that future generations will not forget, in the **Dallas Memorial Center for the Holocaust** at 7900 Northhaven.

Other outings for the whole family include a visit to the **Frontiers of Flight Museum** to review the history of aviation with artifacts from balloon launches to the space program, the *Hindenberg*, and today's stealth bomber. Then take them to **Medieval Times** to enjoy the pageantry of a feast and breathtaking exhibition of horsemanship, ending with a jousting tournament, at 2021 N. Stemmons Freeway (I-35 E). Also set aside a day at the **Dallas Zoo** with award-winning exhibits, including Wilds of Africa, Gorilla Conservation Research Center, the Forest Aviary, and the Chimpanzee Forest. They also have a lot of snakes in the Reptile Discovery Center, which is—my favorite—hands on!

Be sure to view the amazing Dallas skyline, especially after dark when it is outlined in neon, but be careful as you gawk because you need to get on the notorious "mixmaster" to see it.

Foat Wuth

≥ ★ ≤

There was a time when some considered Fort Worth to be something of a "country cousin" to the mega-TV star to its east. But with a beautifully restored, revitalized downtown, museums, a world-class concert hall, an impressive convention center, and the historic district that celebrates the lifestyle of the "true west," this cosmopolitan cow town is in a class of its own.

If you are headed to Fort Worth, you are going to the city "where the West begins." You and your family may want to invest in western wear; because you really will see lots of boots and Wranglers in Cowtown, and you may want to blend. At elegant events you will see the "cowboy tux," which is a combination of starched jeans, vest, and tailed tux jacket, worn with hat and shined boots. Casual attire is accepted almost everywhere, and there are attractions for the whole family.

Your first stop simply must be the **Fort Worth Stockyards** on East Exchange Avenue. Here is where you can get outfitted with the latest in western wear, eat in a wide variety of restaurants, view western art, and really get a feel of the Old West. Take a nine-mile round-trip ride on the **Tarantula Railroad** steam excursion line that rambles through the Trinity River Valley.

Check out the **Livestock Exchange Building** that was built in 1904 as offices for livestock traders and now houses the **Stockyards Collection Museum**. There is also live rodeo at the **Cowtown Coliseum** on Saturday nights from April to September.

Then set aside some time—it will take a while—to have a cold drink and tour the world's largest honkytonk, **Billy Bob's Texas**. This place is amazing, with top country performers, two huge dance floors, and even live indoor rodeo.

On another day follow the red brick road to the **Cultural District**, in the 3000 block of Camp Bowie. Here you will find four outstanding museums: **The Amon Carter**, with works by major nineteenth- and twentieth-century American artists; the **Fort Worth Museum of Science and History** featuring **KIDSPACE, Omni Theater**, **Noble Planetarium**, and **DinoDig** where you can dig for dinosaur bones; **Cattleman's Museum** for a history of the cattle industry in Texas with cowboy and ranch artifacts. Rounding out the four is the incredible **Kimble Art Museum** with a world-class collection of art by the old masters that has been described as "the world's best small museum."

And plan an evening in **Sundance Square**, named for the Sundance Kid—as in "Butch Cassidy and ..." for art, performing arts, shopping, dining, and exciting night life.

For the crowning arts achievement, you simply must visit the exceptional new concert hall that has been named one of the *five* great halls *in the world*, the **Nancy Lee and Perry R. Bass Performance Hall**. Ed Bass, who named the hall in honor of his parents, has been responsible for creating Sundance Square. Here you can enjoy pop or classical music, theater, and ballet.

Take the kids to the **Fort Worth Zoo**, which has gained world recognition and acclaim from *National Geographic*, *Southern Living*, and *USA Today*. They will also enjoy the **Log Cabin Village** with live demonstrations of the early settler activities.

Big and Beautiful on Buffalo Bayou

≳ ★ ≲

Houston is a sprawling, powerful, almost muscular, freeway-driven, lush, massive city with a space-age skyline that almost belies its sensitive, artistic character. I grew up believing that it took everybody at least forty-five minutes to get anywhere. The tropical Houston climate—hot and damp—meant that before everything was air-conditioned, nobody had good hair days. I ironed my hair and set it on orange juice cans and sprayed it with gobs of hair spray. By the time I got to wherever I was going, my hair was plastered to my sweaty forehead in tight ringlets. With the advent of frigid interiors, this is no longer a great problem.

Downtown Houston is a lively area sprinkled with charming cafes and clubs, and lots of folk live right in the middle of things in loft-living homes like the Rice Lofts. After dark the nightlife wakes up the town with every kind of music, lots of dancing, and theaters galore.

More than twenty Houston restaurants have been featured in such magazines as *Gourmet*, and the Zagat Restaurant survey says that Houstonians eat out more than those in any other city, including New York City!

Mom and I used to catch the bus and ride to downtown and spend the day shopping. Now there are cute little trolley cars to ride around, and shopping is an incredible experience, with **Foley's Downtown**, the oldest store in Houston. The **Park Shops** in **Houston Center** houses many trend-setting stores. **Uptown**, at the corner of Westheimer Road and Post Oak, features **The Gallereria**. Here you will find the famous **Neiman-**

Marcus, **Saks Fifth Avenue**, and **Tiffany & Company**. Then shop on at the **Highland Village Shopping Center** just east, which features **Williams-Sonoma** and the **Pottery Barn**.

When I think of Houston I smell pine. **Rice Village** still has that aroma as it is a charming neighborhood offering bistros and stores and featuring trendy clothes and art galleries

The **Houston Heights** is a center for antiques shopping where unique items can be found. Also check out **Old Town Spring**, the **Conroe Outlet Center**, and the **Lone Star State Factory Store**.

And I remember art classes at the **Museum of Fine Arts** and my first stage production at the world-famous **Nina Vance Alley Theater**, which is now an ultramodern facility that the *New York Times* called "one of the most striking theaters in the world."

Also in the downtown **Houston Civic Center** you will find the **Jesse H. Jones Hall for Performing Arts**, the **Sam Houston Coliseum and Music Hall**, and the strikingly beautiful **Wortham Center**, which boasts the Houston Grand Opera and Houston Ballet and other performing arts groups. In the center of the Civic Center is the commemorative **Tranquillity Park**, which honors the Apollo flights with rocket-like towers spilling water into the truly tranquil pool covering two city blocks.

Other attractions include the **Space Center Houston** where you get an up-close, personal look at space travel history. Your family will also enjoy the **Orange Show House**, which is kind of hard to describe. The **Menil Museum** houses the extensive collection of John and Dominique de Menil, which ranges from Byzantine to contemporary works.

Galveston

> ☆

When I was small, sometimes Daddy would come home from work on a Friday and holler, "Pack your suits, we're needing sand in our toes!" and we were off to Galveston. We'd get good and sunburned, eat lots of Gulf shrimp at Guido's, and walk the cool beach after dinner. This beautiful jewel in the sun has thirty-two miles of beach and lots of historical bounty.

The Karankawa Indians were established here first, and then the pirate Jean Lafitte established a settlement in 1817. The hurricane storm of 1900 wiped the island clean, killing more than 5,000 people. But Galveston rebuilt and, protected by a ten-mile seawall, has sustained many storms since then.

Be sure not to miss the incredibly beautiful **Bishop's Palace**. This was built as a private home and later bought by the Galveston-Houston diocese for the bishop. The **Moody Mansion and Museum** was owned by Texas entrepreneur W. L. Moody Jr. until his death in 1954. Another must-see is **Moody Gardens**. The whole family will enjoy the ten-story **Rain Forest Pyramid** that replicates the rain forests with waterfalls, cliffs, exotic fish, and birds.

Buenos Dias, Y'all

≳ ★ ≲

San Antonio is the ultimate in tourist destinations and truly offers so many wonderful experiences that you and your family will want to spend as much vacation time as possible. If you live in Texas, you know that this fantastic experience is only a few hours away and sure to please on weekend getaways.

In 1691 the remote Yanaguana Indian camp on the river (in what was then Mexico) was discovered by a Spanish explorer and a Franciscan padre on the feast day of St. Anthony. Thus the name "San Antonio." Later the Mission San Antonio de Valero (the Alamo) was built, and a "Texian" community was established. Mexico won its freedom from Spain, but Texans wanted to be independent and that started the Texas Revolution. The Battle of the Alamo in 1836 was fought and lost by a small group who held out for thirteen days. "Remember the Alamo" became the war cry that brought about victory and Texas Independence. History rings, energy sings—all calling you to visit, soon!

This is a city that seems to have a musical score playing at all times. With an incredible kaleidoscope of colorful cultures, the city literally dances to the various rhythms that collide yet complement—one trip will never be enough. From the missions to the River Walk, from the professional sports to the theme parks, from Tex-Mex to haute cuisine—music, laughter, and amazement await.

The rich Spanish and Mexican heritage is evident in the beautiful old missions. Just pick up a map for the **Mission Trail** at the Visitor Information Center at 317

147

Alamo Plaza and transport yourself into the past. The **Institute of Texan Cultures** represents twenty-six ethnic and cultural groups in an amazing variety of displays. It also offers a multimedia show several times a day.

No trip to San Antonio would be complete without a long, lazy visit to the beautifully appointed **River Walk**. Here you can have a drink or a complete meal at one of the scenic little sidewalk cafes, shop in unique boutiques and art/gift shops, and even stay in one of the lovely hotels that line the Paseo del Rio. Hop on a river taxi and cruise down the river as folks on the shore wave. Passing slowly, you will be entertained by music and dancers. You will learn to know the difference between tejano and conjunto music. It is hard to believe that a modern city bustles just one level above this beautiful retreat. Popular cabarets offer a wide variety of entertainment, and there is even a **Planet Hollywood** and a **Hard Rock Cafe**. Take advantage of one of the riverboat cruises, and you will truly feel you have been transported to "a whole other country," and you may just want to stay!

The kids will enjoy **Ripley's Believe It or Not!** with more than five hundred oddities, the **Children's Museum**, the **H.E.B. Science Treehouse** at the **Witte Museum**, the **San Antonio Zoo**, and **Sea World of Texas** with "Shamu the Whale" and head-spinning rides. **Fiesta Texas** is a Six Flags Theme Park that is all about the Lone Star State. It includes the very scary Poltergeist coaster, the Lone Star Lagoon, and a wonderful musical.

Visit the **McNay Art Museum** housed in the elegant home of the artist and the **Nelson A. Rockefeller Center for Latin American Art** at the **San Antonio Museum of Art**.

Finally see the **Alamo**. Your kids may be surprised as mine were that it is "so small" as my daughter said. Established in 1718 it was the first of the five missions founded in San Antonio in order to Christianize and educate resident Indians. The church structure in midtown was abandoned by 1836 and is known as the "Cradle of Texas Liberty." In front of the Alamo is the **Alamo Cenotaph**, a monument dedicated to those who lost their lives there. Their names are inscribed in marble in the monument designed by the eminent Italian turned Texan, Pompeo Coppini.

"A Whole Other Country"
—Almost Really

⋛ ★ ⋚

El Paso, the "City in the Sun," is Texas' westernmost city with neighboring Juarez, Chihuahua, across the border in Mexico. If you are in El Paso in the spring, you can join in the Thanksgiving festivities. That's right; the locals say that the first celebration was twenty-three years before the Pilgrims shared their din-din. The city is named for the ancient mountain pass in which it resides. The city is a very popular tourist destination.

To really see the city, plan to take the **Downtown El Paso Walking Tour**, which takes place on the first Saturday of the month. A tour guide will bring to life the colorful history of this exciting and often riotous city. The El Paso of old was a haven for gamblers and gunfighters with Texas Rangers and U.S. marshals hot on their trails. Back then it was known as the Six-Gun Capital of the World. There was a saloon on every corner and raucous wild nightlife. Tours are held each month except on holidays. You only need to have four people for a tour, and it is certainly worth your time.

The oldest community in what is now Texas is the Tigua Indian Reservation: **Ysleta del Sur Pueblo**, which was established in 1681 by refugees from a terrible uprising that ran off Spanish and Christian Indians from what is now New Mexico. Visitors to the Tigua Indian community today will discover a rich educational experience at this museum, and the restaurant serves up genuine gorditas, red and green chili, and Indian bread. Here you can buy some authentic arts and crafts including their famous adobe-oven baked pottery.

Viva El Paso! is an outdoor drama that documents the history of the area. Corpus Christi de la Isleta is the oldest mission in Texas, and you can take a **Trolley on a Mission** tour that allows you to visit the reservation and missions during the summer.

This is also a great time to cross into Mexico. U.S. and Canadian citizens are not required to show papers when traveling to Juarez if they are going to stay less than 72 hours. *Bien venidos!*

There are certainly many other cities in Texas that you will want to visit, and I did not leave anyone out intentionally. Amarillo, Lubbock, Wichita Falls, Corpus Christi, Beaumont, Midland/Odessa, and Bryan/College Station all offer great attractions and dining. These are just the ones I have traveled to recently or know about though dear friends. I am planning trips to many others and hope to write about them in the future. Have fun traveling around our state and be sure to tell your friends.

Small Towns Worth Your Visit

It is my dream to take a weekend every month and visit a small town with a local to give me the real scoop. There are so many it would take a lifetime to do it right. I do know about some sweet spots that you might want to venture out of the cities to find. When you visit, strike up a conversation with a shopkeeper, restaurateur, or vintner. They will fill you in on the local history, and you may just make a friend.

Glen Rose is a pretty town with a lot to offer a tourist. Take the whole family as this is really a family place. The must-see is the **Fossil Rim Wildlife Center** were you can spend hours enjoying close encounters with animals not frequently seen in Texas. You haven't lived until you have been "slimed" while feeding a giraffe. You can drive your own vehicle or tour in an open van with a guide. This gorgeous park also offers overnight accommodations; this is not roughing it at all. The tents look like what you would find on an African safari, but they are heated and air-conditioned and come with a private bath. This is also a great educational experience as the center is in the forefront of saving endangered wildlife species. If you have more time, stay at the **Inn On The River** and take fly fishing lessons and catch a performance of *The Promise* outdoor drama.

If you aren't already a fan of Larry McMurtry, the author of *Lonesome Dove*, *The Last Picture Show*, *Texasville*, and *Duane's Depressed*, you should be ashamed of yourself. If you go to **Archer City**, you can visit **Booked Up!**, his very own bookstore in his very own hometown. The store features rare and lovingly used books, McMurtry's passion. There are even plans to restore the **Royal Theatre** as a center for the performing arts. This town was the inspiration for *The Last Picture Show*, and the movie was actually filmed there.

The warm town of **Comfort** in the Hill Country is home to **Arlene's Cafe**, where you will feel right at home. Be sure to have some melt-in-your-mouth yeast biscuits. *Southern Living* magazine said Comfort was "like a candy counter for antiques lovers." So enjoy shopping at **Faltin & Company**, which is a family business featuring quality furnishings and Andrew Wyeth prints. Continue your tour with the **Comfort Antique Mall** or the exotic **Wilson-Clements Antiques and Gifts**.

Hico is a lovely town that boasts it was a hideout for Billy the Kid. The renovated historic downtown features interesting shops like **Cowboy Art**, **Lonnie and Mabel's**, the **Wiseman House**, and the fabulous **Lilly's** Mexican restaurant. We live close and eat there often, but folks drive out from the Metroplex to enjoy Tex-Mex and a margarita.

Take a short drive southwest from Fort Worth and you will find a very friendly town on **Lake Granbury** that bears the same name. **Granbury** has a number of good restaurants. We enjoy **Hennington's Texas Cafe** and the **Pasta House**. Then stroll around the Victorian square for a varied shopping experience—fashions, antiques, books, quilts, and collectibles—and stop for an ice cream at **Rinky Tinks**. The **Granbury Opera House** offers up professional live theater year round featuring performers from around the state and nation. This town offers a great get-away weekend of sightseeing and relaxing fun. I always take my out-of-town guests for a visit.

Jefferson lures antique shoppers from Dallas and Shreveport with a wide selection of stores. The **Terry House** and the **Old Mill Antiques** flea market will keep any shopper happy. When you are tired and hungry drop into the **Stillwater Inn** for elegant fare cooked up by owner/chef Bill Stewart.

Clifton has been officially designated as the Norwegian Capital of Texas by the state legislature. This town was settled by Norwegian and German immigrants in the mid-1800s. Here you can explore the great collection of pioneer articles at the **Bosque Memorial Museum** in the **Norse Historic District**. This town is also home to the **Bosque Conservatory**, which is a center for both the visual and the performing arts. Clifton has been designated as one of the top one hundred small art communities in the nation.

To happen upon the community of **Round Top** you might never suspect that it is home to an international music festival, but that is only the beginning. The shopping here is great with stores like **Porch Office Antiques** and the **Painted Pony**. My Houston friend recommends **Royer's Round Top Cafe** on the square for a bite to eat.

There are few small towns that can claim fame for a more important staple of the American diet than **Athens**. Named for either the center of early culture in Greece or the city in Georgia, there is no argument here that this is the Home of the Hamburger! The Uncle Flecher Davis Home of the Hamburger Cook-Off is held each September. You may also venture to New York (Texas) to sample free cheesecake or stay the night at the bed and breakfast and have a gourmet dinner on Saturday nights at the **New York (Texas) Cheesecake Outlet**.

Waxahachie offers the veteran shopper up-scale and down-scale buys and everything in between. The imposing courthouse is surrounded by shops on the square. You will also love the **Webb Gallery** with its cast-iron facade that welcomes you into Texas's largest folk art gallery where you can see a variety of art works. The **Dove's Nest** will be ready to serve you a delightful lunch or dinner on the weekends.

Boerne is a town rich with historic significance in the scenic Hill Country where you can visit the **Guadalupe River State Park** and enjoy the bluebonnets in the spring. Located just a few minutes north of San Antonio, the town was named for Ludwig Boerne who inspired its German founders. You can plan a family vacation at **Guadalupe River Ranch** or a hunting/fishing trip at **Joshua Creek Ranch**. The **Tapatio Spring Resort and Conference Center** offers excellent amenities and features the **Blue Heron Restaurant**.

XIT was once a ranch that was twenty-seven miles wide and almost two hundred miles long—three million acres owned by some Yankees. **Dalhart** hosts the **XIT Rodeo and Reunion** every summer. Check out the **Empty Saddle Monument** downtown and visit the **XIT Museum**, which records the history of this vast ranch that was home to many cowboys and their families for years.

Just north of the Metroplex lies the Wine Capital of Texas, **Grapevine**. This town is home to four wineries that operate tasting rooms. These include the **Delaney Vineyards**, featuring a French-style state-of-the-art winery; the **Homestead Winery**, which in located in the Historic District; **La Buena Vida Vineyards**, featuring demonstrations; and **La Bodega Winery**, with the first ever wine tasting room located in an international airport. The third weekend in April, Grapevine hosts the **New Vintage Wine & Art Festival** with wine seminars, gourmet Chef's Brunch, and art display.

Roanoke, north of Fort Worth, boasts the best fried chicken around, which is served at **Babe's**. With a sign that says "Texas ain't no place for amateurs" and its name in neon lights, your meal can be served with great sides of mashed potatoes, gravy, creamed corn, and biscuits.

On down south between Austin and San Antonio is an artist community that attracts tourists with unusual arts and crafts, great food, and music. After a day of shopping, stop in at the **Cypress Creek Cafe** in **Wimberly**. Here you can eat in the homey cafe up front and then retire to the bar to hear folk and country music and even take to the dance floor for a turn or two.

The oldest town in the state is **Nacogdoches**. The word for friend, "tejas," was the Nacogdoches Indians' word and the origin of the name Texas. Visit the **Millard's Crossing** historic village just north of the town. The **Stone Fort Museum** is a replica made from the actual stones from the original building. This is also the home of Stephen F. Austin State University.

Kerrville in the beautiful Texas Hill Country is home to the **Cowboy Artist of America Museum**. This museum is dedicated to the celebration of the Western artwork in paint, bronze, and stone. Educational programs promote a better understanding of Western heritage and art. Check out the museum store for limited edition prints and gifts.

Of course **Kingsville** is the place to go to learn more about the massive **King Ranch** founded by Captain Richard King back in 1853. Downtown discover the **King**

Ranch Museum with historic ranch memorabilia including carriages, cars, and saddles. Visit the **King Ranch Saddle Shop** for leatherwear and goods.

Pack your flip-flops and your swimsuit and head south to **Port Aransas** on **Mustang Island** for fishing, birding, shelling, shopping, dining, or just plain relaxing. My sister went down and never came back—well, she plans to retire there anyway!

I can't leave out my stompin' grounds. In **Stephenville** go shopping at the **Chicken House Flea Market**, open most weekends in the summer, enjoy country music at the **Cross Timbers Country Opry** house (stars on the way up like Leanne Rhymes have played here), see **Moola** on the square, and have lunch at the fabulous **Cafe Trifles**. Do some shopping at **All Seasons** gift shop on the North Loop, and then dance the night away at **City Limits** where the big acts play.

Finally, the town that my great-grandmother Gran "Babe" Keith settled in so long ago is **Dublin**. On your way from Stephenville stop at the **Hoka Hey Fine Arts Foundry & Gallery** to view world famous bronze casting, have some fine barbecue at **Woody's**, and say "Hi!" to Woody and Shelly as you shop at **Woody's 377 Trade Days** weekend flea market. In town shop with Sara at the **Checkerboard** and next door at **The Golden Butterfly** for fashions and jewelry, look for works of art at the **Art Gallery in Dublin**, and then have a float at the **Dr Pepper Museum & Old Doc's Soda Shop**. You can also take the tour of the oldest Dr Pepper Bottling Company in the world, which is conveniently located next door. The **Dublin Museum** is filled with interesting memories of Dublin's rich heritage.

Funny Texans
(I'm Related to Most of Them)

⋛ ★ ⋚

Texans love to make each other laugh. My mother, Dixie, is one of the funniest people I know. She was born in Dallas on one of those cold days some eighty years ago. "They told me a man froze to death on the viaduct that night. I always remembered sitting in a diaper, up front with the doctor, who was driving to my house to deliver me, like milk or eggs."

She says it is difficult to be funny out in public because "Then people expect it of you, and the next time they see you, you've got to top yourself." Once she was headed into the H-E-B and walked by a little lady who was bent over checking out the flowering plants display. Mom leaned over to her and whispered, "You pull your car around, I'll create a diversion, and you can just load 'em up." The little lady 'bout lost her balance laughing.

While Mom was waiting at the mechanic's one time, he asked her to please catch the phone while he went back out in the garage. The phone didn't ring. He returned and asked, "Did I get any calls?" Mom shot back really quick, "Just some woman, said she was your wife and wanted to know who I was. I just told her I was your sweet patootie."

Mom also told me about a small family from far out East Texas who had never been more than a few miles from their farm. Having inherited a small fortune, they drove all the way to Dallas for the first time. They found their way to a mall, and the father and young son decided to actually go in; but the mother was frightened and decided to stay in the truck.

The father and son were overwhelmed by what they saw in the mall. They sat on a bench to catch their breath and began watching an incredible wall that could open and close and had blinking lights above the opening. They watched as a very old woman with a stooped back and a walker waited and when the wall opened, haltingly made her way through. The wall closed. The father and son watched as the lights flashed and blinked. The wall opened and out stepped a beautiful young woman. The father said quietly to his son, "Boy, go get your mother."

I was at Micky's hair salon one afternoon when she was trying to get Walter to carry some chickens over to Sandy's place. Walter, a real Texas gentleman, said, "No, now, I'm sorry, but I just don't like chickens. I never have. I never will. I don't even eat chicken." Conversation turned to other topics like who used to be married to whom and the weather. Sandy cut Walter's hair telling him he'd lost some more. Micky, laughing, said she didn't think you were supposed to talk to a client like that. Sandy said she was just telling the truth. We all chatted up a storm, and Walter was headed for the door when somebody asked after Micky's cat. Walter said, "How is that old cat, I like him. If you ever thought about giving that cat away, I'd take him. I like cats—and dogs—and cows and most animals for that matter. But I just don't like chickens."

My grandmother, Dixie's mom, was a real wit who peppered her conversation with nuggets of advice. One of her best was what you should pray before entering a social engagement. "I always say, 'Dear Lord, please don't let me leave here today with the sound of my own voice ringing in my ears.'"

Granddaddy might not have been the first to say, "Don't ever ask a man where he's from. If he's from Texas, he'll tell you; and if not, you don't want to embarrass him," but he's the first I heard say it.

Some stories didn't start out to be funny but were just slips of the tongue that are repeated for generations as family entertainment. My mother-in-law was famous for some great ones. One rainy day she was driving to church and saw a friend walking, so she pulled over. She hollered, "Now, Louise May, you get out from under that piano right now and get in this car." Her friend laughed so hard she almost couldn't get the umbrella in the car.

She was a lovely woman—attractive, bright, quite a fashion plate, and kept a beautiful home—but she was a notoriously bad cook. She loved trying new recipes, but they were often inedible. As a young bride I was very nervous about having her to dinner. As my father-in-law and husband wolfed down the lasagna that I had prepared, she poked at her plate tentatively and asked, "Now, son, what was that I-talian casserole dish called that I had to feed to the cats?"

I remember vividly the morning when I asked if she was feeling well, as she was rubbing her neck. She answered sincerely, "Well, my word, I think I must have slept with a necked crook."

Her sister was also a delight for impromptu, unintentional comedy. Once at a large church convention she was introduced to a minister from out of state. Upon hearing his very familiar last name she bubbled, "Well, I don't believe it—that's my last name, too." Then red-faced she admitted, "Oh, no it's not—that's my sister's last name."

My daddy had a very dry wit, and folks weren't always sure that he was being funny on purpose. Usually he was. Every time my mother would prepare a beautiful meal and we sat down at the table, he would say, "Well, I wonder what the enlisted men are having tonight!"

He was always making us kids get our "tickle boxes turned upside down." When we brought friends with us to church, he would start priming us early for our trip to Luby's for lunch. The little lady who served the salad had a strong Yankee accent that Daddy thought was a hoot. "Now, don't you kids dare to laugh when the salad lady says, "Sellet plis, sellet plis." By the time we pulled into the parking lot, we would be near hysterics. Mom, too. On the way up to the line he would implore, "Really now I mean it, don't laugh." As the little lady turned her attention to the first of us and said the magic words, we would dissolve into gales of laughter and shakily point to the fruit filled Jell-O. It worked every time.

When I went off to college, I got mail from my daddy once a week like clockwork. It always had the same note, "Just thought I'd drop you a check to see how you are. Love, Dad." He was not a tall man and was frequently teased about being short. His retort was always, "Whadaya mean, I could eat soup off your head."

Dad's all-time favorite joke went something like this: A woman called the police and excitedly reported that a man was strutting around on his back porch naked in her full view! The police responded and asked to see where this display was taking place. "Right out my bathroom window," she said. The two rather tall officers entered the small bathroom and looked out the window. Not seeing anything, they asked the woman if she was sure she had seen this naked man out this window. "Of course, I'm sure," she replied, "But you have to get up on the toilet, stick your head out the window, and lean to the left, and you'll see him!"

My friend Ann is no Texan for sure! She's from Boston and has lived in California so long she thinks sushi is food and can wither a wine steward with a glare at thirty paces. She is always e-mailing me Texas stuff that she thinks is funny, but not long ago she sent a good one.

Three Texans went down to Mexico one night, got drunk, and woke up in jail. They found out that they were going to be executed for crimes they couldn't remember. The first one was strapped in the electric chair and was asked for his last words.

"I am from the University of Texas School of Law, and I believe in the eternal power of Justice to intervene on the part of the innocent," he said. They threw the switch and nothing happened, so they figured the law was on this guy's side and let him go.

The second one was strapped in and said, "I am from the Baylor School of Divinity, and I believe in the almighty power of God to intervene on behalf of the innocent." They threw the switch and nothing happened. They figured God didn't want this guy to die, so they let him go.

The last one was strapped in and said, "Well I'm a Texas Aggie Electrical Engineer, and I'll tell you right now you'll never electrocute anybody if you don't connect those two wires."

Mom's all-time favorite joke is also an Aggie joke. You have to understand that Mom loves A&M, watches all of their games, and believes my finest accomplishment was landing myself an Aggie. She tells about the two Aggies who were driving down Highway 183 when the driver turned on the radio. The traffic reporter said, "If you are on 183 watch out, there's a car driving against the traffic." The other Aggie said, "One car, hell, there's thousands of 'em."

Loyalty

≥ ★ ≤

Texans are loyal. We are loyal to our families, friends, hairdressers, mechanics, banks, brand names, automakes, football teams, hometowns, disinfectants, personal products, churches, universities, newspapers, and fish bait. We will drive farther and pay more for an item that might be of lower quality if we are buying from a friend.

I have friends who all swear by "Burt," the mechanic who has a place in a small town some twenty miles out from the city. He has at all times at least one of their vehicles in his shop with the hood up or on the rack with parts laid all over the ground. You nearly always find Burt with a cold Dr Pepper in his hand as he's wiping the sweat from his brow with an oily rag. Whether you ask or not, he's complaining about trying to get a part. He's called everybody he personally knows, but he's got some leads on that out-of-date part. Folks stop by two or three times a day to chat and poke in or under their cars or trucks and have a Dr Pepper. Then too, Burt spends a lot of time telling folks to check back in a couple of days and maybe he'll get to it later. He walks from one frozen metal sculpture to the next and barks out an occasional instruction to his nephew, Junior. Of course, Junior is eating his third bean burrito while talking into the phone as he's telling somebody to check back later. Burt's usual solution to most problems is carburetor cleaner or WD-40. You'd better not question Burt's abilities, or somebody will tell you, "There's nobody who's a better mechanic in three counties. When he gets it fixed, it's fixed."

I had a lady tell me one time that she had gone to the same beauty parlor for twenty-three years. I said she must have really liked her beautician. She said, "No, I've always hated the way Sammi Sue does my hair. She sorta pinches my scalp when she rolls me up, and her perms always poop out before the week is out." I couldn't imagine why she stayed with her. She explained the woman was her next-door neighbor's daughter. "My neighbor passed away four years ago; but I can't stop now, or it'll hurt Sammi Sue's feelings."

Families are very loyal to their members. This includes aunts, uncles, cousins, grandparents, nieces, nephews, and all. For example, if one family has a son who is a quarterback for his high school football team, then everybody has to go to all the games. I think the rule is that if you are within a five-hundred-mile radius, you have to go. You have to be at all the games, because his mother will be taking roll.

Texans are loyal to their friends. When you have a Texas friend, you've got a friend for life. When they invite you to visit, they aren't just blowin,' and they will show you a great time. I know of a Texas family whose son started writing to a pen pal in Australia. Soon all the kids in both families were writing and faxing. The moms got into the act, and then they were burning up the phone lines. The dads even started swapping info and asking questions. The Aussies got a chance to visit the U.S. for the first time ever. They were to have nine weeks to travel, so the Texans invited them to stay with them—for the whole time. The Texas mom said, "I told them that everything they could want to see was right here!" It all started with a letter.

Chili for the Texas Soul: Random Acts of Kindness

⋛ ★ ⋚

I hadn't been back in Texas very long when I was vividly reminded of what sets our state apart from the rest of the world more than anything else. I was sitting in 5 o'clock traffic in the little town of Cedar Park on Highway 183 when I realized that the vehicle at the light was not moving. Since I was about seven cars back, there was really nowhere to go. All of a sudden a tall cowboy, boots and hat and all, appeared and started directing cars to move back and over. He then helped the owner of the stalled truck push it off the road and into a parking lot. As traffic resumed I watched to see where this hero had come from. He jogged down the grassy knoll to the convenience store parking lot and retrieved his cold drink and burrito from the roof of his truck. I was astounded. This guy had just gotten his supper, saw the problem, and took it upon himself to solve it. A simple random act of kindness. You'd never get that in L. A.

It is true that if you have car trouble in Texas, you needn't panic. Before you know it a truck will show up with a couple of young men who will fix whatever is wrong with your vehicle and take only a thank-you as payment—better than AAA with a warm fuzzy feeling.

When I asked my friend Micky about random acts of kindness, she said, " That's easy, the lady who found me a screw!" Turns out her husband, Ted, sent her into town to match a screw he needed for some dairy equipment. She went to an old shop where Mrs. Billie Morgan began the search for the screw. "I know I have one of those," she said with confidence. An hour and a half later, opening many little drawers and boxes, sure enough she found it and a washer to match. Ted went into town several days later and stopped by to thank Mrs. Morgan. She asked him if he'd like to go to the restaurant next door to grab a cup of coffee. "Ted admitted he didn't have any money on him to pay for the coffee, so she loaned him $10," Micky explained. Then when their hot water heater broke down in the middle of the night, Mr. Morgan came out to fix it and told Micky and Ted to get some sleep. When they got up the water heater was fixed, and Mr. Morgan had herded the cows in and started the milking! You wouldn't get that in California.

My daughter, Alisa Robin, and a friend had stopped at an all-night diner while making a long trip before Christmas one year. She said the waitress was about full-term pregnant and working so hard and being so nice to everyone. They had their coffee and a bite to eat and were struck by how this young waitress continued to have a smile for everyone. They noticed she was very tired and that she stopped briefly now and then to rub her aching back. They thanked her profusely as they left, and when she picked up her tip she found twenty-five dollars. My daughter said, "I just knew it might make her holiday a little better."

Grocery Shopping Kindnesses

As a newbee or visitor to our fair state, you need to be informed of the grocery store etiquette in Texas. I know that in most parts of the country, going for food supplies is a painful chore to be endured as briefly and determinedly as a root canal. Folks trek with grudging purpose up and down isles, grabbing items, and scratching lists with eyes on the distasteful task at hand. Not so in Texas. Grocery shopping is a social affair involving as much meeting, greeting, networking, political commentary, and sharing of jokes and recent operations as a huge family reunion or Shriners' convention.

Before selecting a basket, make sure you have taken care of all older persons, women with small children, and certainly pregnant women's basket needs. In produce be prepared to discuss comparative quality and price of fruits and vegetables with perfect strangers. Be ready to recommend better sources if you have seen such at the competing H-E-B or Piggly Wiggly. If no one is choosing tomatoes, pass them up. You may be shamed into a drive to one of the shoppers' favorite produce stands in a neighboring community. Don't be offended if folks peruse your cart and ask what you are planning for dinner. They are just being friendly.

If you are on the tall side, be ready to fetch and reach canned goods from top shelves. If you don't wear glasses, you will be called upon to read labels for the sight impaired. If you see a wandering, confused senior citizen, offer assistance. If you are a wandering, confused senior citizen, rest assured someone will help you find your favorite brand of tomato sauce. If you are young and strong, you will be asked to hoist heavy bags of kitty litter and barbecue briquettes from lower shelves into baskets for the not so young and strong.

Picking out a greeting card can, and often does, lead to viewing photos of grandchildren and discussions of genealogy. Only venture into baby product aisles if you have planned to spend the greater portion of your day at the store. The same advice applies to the entire pharmacy section, as detailed discussions of gallbladder surgeries can be lengthy.

At the checkout line, the shopper with the fewest items gets to go first. And don't panic if you come up a little short of cash; folks in line will take up a collection and cover you. If the wait in line gets a little long, you will get to meet everyone around you and play the "do you know" game to pass the time. For example: "We just moved here from Arizona." "Oh, well then do you know the Jim Bob Whites?"

My friend Pam says it was hard to get used to the pace here after moving from California. "I was in line one time behind a woman with a fussy toddler. The cashier took the baby, left the register, walked out the front door, and bought the child a soda pop from the machine, while the woman wrote out her check. I couldn't believe it. I hadn't adjusted yet and was, of course, in a hurry."

The teen who grabs your basket of bagged groceries and heads for the door is not a thief, but an employee who expects no tip. Amazing! You don't get that in California.

And If You Got Real Trouble

≷ ★ ≶

Little kindnesses like how folks wave at you and say "Howdy!" even if they don't know you add up, and when real trouble rears its ugly head, Texans respond.

Cecilia and her husband have been born-again Texans twice. She told me about their first move when she was a young mom of a six-month-old. "We didn't have a washing machine or a dryer." They had just moved into student housing. "I washed four loads of clothes at the laundromat—with lots of diapers of course. I brought them home to line-dry to save money." During the night a big storm blew in, unbeknownst to the exhausted mommy. The next morning she answered a knock at the door. It was her downstairs neighbor to tell her that he had gathered her laundry and dried and folded it for her.

On their second move to Texas they were unloading the large U-Haul with no help. They didn't know anyone in their new home of Bowie. "Three guys came by who were doing home visits for their church. They started helping and called some other church members, who all pitched in until we were totally moved in." Amazing? No, it's Texas.

In another U-Haul story, Cecilia was driving her baby to the doctor's office, when she ran out of gas. She was out on a lonely farm road and saw no choice but to put the baby on her hip and start walking. "I didn't get more than a few yards when a couple in a U-Haul passed me going the other way. They made a U-turn in that U-Haul and came back for me and the baby." They took her into town, got her gas, and drove her back to her car!

Pam hadn't lived in Texas very long when she was driving her girls to school one day and had a blowout. She was pretty scared to be alone on a deserted road with her little girls, but in less than three minutes five men had stopped to help change the tire, including one gentleman about eighty years old. "I had never seen anything like that before!"

That story reminded Sandy of the time she was headed to Kari's house with her baby and a pitcher of margaritas to enjoy some much needed R&R on a cold afternoon. In a frightening turn of events, her car slid off the road. "Within minutes an old guy showed up in a scary beat-up truck. He loaded me, the baby, and the margaritas into that truck and drove me all the way to Kari's.

Kari had no trouble coming up with examples of random kindnesses done to her family after they moved to Texas. She remembers vividly the time when their dairy barn burned, and they needed a place to milk five hundred cows immediately. A neighbor just five miles away, who had sold his herd just a few months earlier, offered his barn—a blessing. But then they were faced with the enormous task of quickly transporting all those cows. Within an hour of the barn burning word was out in her small community, and trailers started lining up next to the burned barn to load cows. Volunteers came from all around to load, haul, herd cattle in and out, and do the actual milking. "Dairymen and neighbors, friends, and people we hardly knew came. Several of the wives helped haul the cattle while the husbands helped sort and milk. There were people there I'd never seen with so much as a spot of dirt on their starched shirts and Wranglers."

The fire happened at noon, and although they normally would have been finished milking by six in the evening, that night they finished after eleven. Yet, people stayed and helped with the morning milking. "I'll never forget the feeling of passing folks on the road that day who were helping with the move to the other barn. Grain companies moved the feed and none asked for payment. When it was time for the move back to our place, they came back again. We knew we were in Texas then."

When Kari was four months pregnant with the last of their four children, she had complications and was confined to bed. With three other children to care for, she didn't know how she would manage. Then the neighbors and some folks at the church found out and started bringing in food and helping with some of the chores around the place. Her son was well into his "terrible twos" and quite a handful back then. "He still remembers all the treats I hid under my bed to pull out and surprise him with. The kids still remember those spaghetti dinners, ham, and other goodies. How can you ever thank those people enough. I made friends I didn't know I had."

Those were the "biggies" for Kari's family. "Made us feel a part of this state and proud to have the neighbors and friends we do—those who care and know what is happening around them and reach out to others. You'd never get that in California."

For my friend Nancy, 1998 started out to be an exciting year. She and her husband, Bob, were planning to open a new business she was really happy about. It was going to be a specialty gift store filled with goodies she would personally select. Plans moved along for a fall opening that assured them a busy holiday season. Nancy couldn't have been more pleased. Then a few weeks before the planned date something happened.

"I was just putting on my lipstick, and I sort of slipped, like my mouth was a little numb. It was weird. Then later that day I almost fell off a ladder, and I thought I'd had a stroke," Nancy says. Bob chimes in, "I was scared when she said 'stroke.'" Bob called a doctor-friend and got her checked out right away. Nancy was diagnosed with Bell's Palsy, and they quickly learned that as frightening as it was, it is not a life-threatening condition. They were told that the condition (facial paralysis) was more than likely temporary. Still Nancy was certainly in no condition to continue the work that was necessary to open the new shop—and she had twenty-five wreaths to finish.

Her anguish was erased when her dear friend drove over one hundred miles from Dallas to take charge. Being the wife of a judge, her friend's holiday and social events calendar was more than full, but all that was set aside. Marsha helped with the shop and incredibly finished all of the wreaths. The shop opened on time. "I think I'd have to say that's one of the very nicest things a Texan ever did for me," a grateful Nancy says.

A Honky-Tonk Love Story

≳ ★ ≲

At my favorite dance hall, the City Limits, there is a lovely lady named Joanne. She sits at "her" table almost every Friday and Saturday night, just to the side of the large dance floor, with a Big Red. She is wearing a colorful flowered outfit, and her hair is freshly done, piled high with curls. As dancers take to the floor so does Joanne— sans partner. With carefully measured steps she glides around the perimeter of the floor in perfect time to the music. Sometimes she dances several in a row. Then she returns to her table and "holds court" as folks drop by to say Hi and see how she is faring tonight. She comes to all the big concerts. If she is not in the house, she is missed. Big name performers look forward to seeing that Joanne is still here.

Sometimes she will dance with one of the young men who check on her, but a partner is not really called for. You see some years back she and her husband used to go out dancing on the weekends. A love for country music and the two-step was a part of the love they shared. Then he passed away. She stayed home for a few months, and then one night she got herself up and went to City Limits. It was like she could breathe again. She started having her hair done again and taking an interest in her outfits for dancing. So you see, she already has a dancing part- ner—she dances with the memory of her husband.

Texas Cuisine

$\stackrel{\scriptstyle \vcenter{}}{}$ ✦ $\stackrel{\scriptstyle \vcenter{}}{}$

Upon my rebirth as a Texan, I was assailed by memories from my childhood. Many of the fondest were food related. I had forgotten my old favorite sandwiches like pimento cheese, egg salad, sliced dill pickles and mayo, grilled cheese, BLTs, banana/peanut butter/raisin, and my all-time favorite, kitchen sink tomato. This last concoction requires fresh Mrs. Baird's white bread, slathered with mayo, and tomatoes sun-warmed straight from the garden. They are so juicy they dribble down your chin and therefore are best eaten over the kitchen sink.

When I moved to New York, I laughed out loud the first time I saw a Yankee prepare a sandwich with butter. And my first Thanksgiving in Colorado, I had a heck of a time finding a can of French fried onions to top my green bean casserole with the cream of mushroom soup. "Are you sure they come in a can, ma'am? I've been working here for years, and I've never heard of them."

Visits to garden club luncheons and church socials reminded me of fruit filled Jell-O molds, tuna noodle casseroles, spicy macaroni and cheese, King Ranch casserole, deviled eggs, and baked beans floating in catsup, brown sugar, and covered in bacon slices. I rediscovered Ranch spaghetti. It's brown not red, like my mamma used to make, with melted cheddar on top. Above all I reveled in the Tex-Mex cuisine that can be replicated nowhere else on the planet. Eating these hot, cheesy, spicy concoctions of tortillas, beans, meat, onions, and peppers with red or green sauces heaped on sizzling platters just makes your scalp perspire.

Native Texans have their taste buds burned out by the time they enter kindergarten. We don't believe we are eating unless we feel the fire, and it makes our eyebrows sweat. If you tell us something is spicy, we'll pour on the hot sauce before we even taste it. When you sit down in a Texas cafe, you will discover that right next to the salt and pepper is catsup, hot sauce, and red pepper flakes. We use 'em all on most everything, which is why we consume vast quantities of iced tea.

We call it "ice tea" and some folks like lots of sugar, or they'll tump in several of those pink or blue packets. I need extra lemon, and we all like it fresh brewed. We drink it year round. I was astounded after I left my home state to discover that my drink of choice was not available everywhere all the time. When it was available, three tiny ice cubes just wouldn't cut it. Other favored drinks include coffee (strong, high speed or decaf), Coke, Pepsi, and Dr Pepper.

We drink coffee all day, and many of us enjoy some of those fancy cappuccinos on occasion. But of a morning, folks require the real thang. Cowboy coffee, roasted over a campfire, served in an enameled cup with half an inch of grounds in the bottom is reason enough to rise with the sun and thank God you're in Texas. They say you need to chunk a horseshoe in the pot. If it sinks, the coffee's not fit to drink.

Folks are mighty divided about the Coke and Pepsi wars, and most will bypass a restaurant that doesn't serve their cola of choice. But most all agree that a cold Dr Pepper, especially the original recipe made with cane sugar, is the nectar of the gods. Growing up we always celebrated the holiday season with hot Dr Pepper poured over a lemon slice and served in china cups. You can get the real brew from the bottling company in Dublin, Texas, founded more than a hundred years ago. While you're there, you can view Pretty Peggy Pepper swinging on the billboard in downtown Dublin at her namesake's park. Yeah, she actually swings.

Many folks, including some state legislators, are confused into thinking that chili is the state dish of Texas. That's just ignorant because chili is served in a *bowl*. No, the Lone Star State's *dish* is chicken-fried steak. You will never find a good one outside our borders unless a misplaced Texan cooks it for you. Larry McMurtry indicated the importance of this "cowboy soul food," in his book *In a Narrow Grave: Essays on Texas*. On the last leg of a trip that took him around the state, he headed for Dalhart.

"It only remained to perform some *acte symbolistique* to give the drive coherence, tie the present to the past. I stopped at a cafe in Dalhart and ordered a chicken-fried steak. Only a rank degenerate would drive 1,500 miles across Texas without eating a chicken-fried steak," he wrote.

This is a sizable steak that gets beat like the devil's wife until it is twice its original size, seasoned just right, and beat some more. Then it is floured, dipped in egg and milk (or buttermilk), and back in the flour. After the steak and your entire kitchen is entirely covered in batter, it is fried in hot oil in an iron skillet until it's golden brown. The edges of the steak should overlap the plate with the cream gravy served on top. The gravy gets made from the pan-drippins with a little flour (cooked like a roux) and milk added and seasoned with salt and pepper. Add some mashed potatoes and a mess of green beans, cooked with onions and bacon, warm biscuits, and—can I get a witness here—this is so good you'll want to slap your pappy!

Some folks tell the story that a diner waitress yelled an order to the cook, "Chicken 'nd fried steak," as two separate orders. The cook misunderstood and created the masterpiece. Certainly the Germans have inspired it with their wiener schnitzel. Although the exact origin may never be known, it gained great popularity during the lean days of the Depression. However it came about, do yourself a favor and get to a great Texas eatery (I like the Broken Spoke and Threadgill's, both in Austin, and the Waco Elite Cafe) and find out what the fuss is all about. Then get adventurous and cook some up at home. I've included chicken-fried steak in the recipe chapter, and don't forget to add paper towels to your ingredient list.

A traditional "bowl of red" Texas chili does not have beans or tomatoes. The red color comes from the chilies. Hot damn! Real chili has good tender chunks of beef or sometimes a mixture of venison and beef. The sauce is often a mix of beef stock, onions, chili powder (special blends), and whatever liquid is available—beer, wine, whiskey, cola, or just plain ol' water. Although there are many chili contests, the Annual World Championship Chili Cook-Off is held on the first Saturday in November in Terlingua. Terlingua is in the Big Bend, which is at least five hundred miles from anywhere you live. You need plenty of space for the five thousand "chili heads" who show up for the oldest cook-off in the state. It is best to arrive in an RV or an airplane since you must camp out. That's a lot of folks for a small town with less than a hundred residents. This great Texas tradition began as a contest between Wick Fowler and H. Allen Smith, a couple of funny guys who made hot bowls of red and battled with quick wit and hilarious observations to the delight of the crowds. At the same time the Chili Appreciation Society International hosts a cook-off with contenders from around the world. The trick to winning one of these events is to make the judges turn bright red, produce steam from their ears, sweat profusely, and smile. But no spitting here—that would be bad.

If the truth be known, most home cooks use tomatoes and beans in the chili they serve their families; a little filler goes a long way to feeding a large family. Ro-Tel tomatoes (stewed tomatoes with chopped green chili peppers) were my grandma's chili secret. Come to think of it without Ro-Tel tomatoes, Velveeta cheese, and cream of mushroom soup, Texas home cuisine would not exist.

Texas also boasts the most succulent seafood and fresh water fish you ever sunk your teeth in. The coast offers up shrimp, oysters, crabs, redfish, and snapper. From Galveston on down into Brazoria County and all the way over to Mexico, you'll find camping areas where the fishing and crabbing is great. For a real adventure try deep-sea fishing. A friend of mine went down to Port Aransas, and her husband just had to try the deep-sea deal. Well, she didn't want to, but they went anyway. He wound up sick as the proverbial dawg, but turned out she was good at it and pulled in a whopper. Rivers, streams, and stock tanks offer catfish, crappie, bass, and crawfish. Though the latter are certainly unfortunately named. Folks across the country are discovering the joy of the mild fish fillets and the "little lobsters" that we grew up calling "crawdads." Farm raising of catfish has made it one of the most popular fish choices with home cooks. You will find fried catfish on menus in many Texas restaurants, and never pass up an invite to a fish fry party.

Barbecue done Texas style is central to our culture. On a drive down most any roadway through any small town or big city, you will be enticed with an array of barbecue joints (some too elegant to be referred to as joints). Some are just an RV with a pit belching smoky wood-flavored aromas and a hand painted sign saying "BBQ." Some of the best barbecue comes with no plate at all, you eat it off butcher paper. It's usually served with sides of baked beans, coleslaw, potato salad, and maybe roasted corn on the cob. Some places give you Texas toast (wide sliced) or just plain white bread to sop up the juices. The meat of choice is beef, usually brisket or ribs, but you will also find great sausage and pork baby-back ribs. Nowadays most places also serve great smoked chicken and turkey. Barbecued turkey legs are a favorite at fairs and festivals. Every man of consequence has a barbecue recipe. Usually he won't tell you the recipe—not to be mean—most don't use an actual recipe. They go by taste and smell and color. Dry rubs and sauces are both used, but inevitably there are peppers involved. We don't tend to do the yellow mops (mustard based) or honey sweet sauces you have in the South, but more a rich, dark tomato-based sauce or a dark red rub. A lot of folks use both.

Any respectable supermarket in Texas will have a dazzling array of peppers. They come fresh with skins shiny red, yellow, green, or dried to a deep mahogany. Jalapeños, poblanos, serranos, cayennes, and habaneros are a few of the wonderful peppers Mexican cuisine has infused into our Tex-Mex cooking. Lots of us eat them raw, but remember, our taste buds are gone.

In the new Texas haute cuisine, peppers show up mixed with kiwi, star fruit, and mangos in "salsas," but we know that real salsa is red or green. Every restaurant has its own special recipe. The really good ones are hot enough to require pitchers of margaritas or Mexican beer. The ploy here is to get you to buy a gallon or two while you're too tipsy to remember whether you liked it or not.

Pecans (pronounced puh-cons, not pee-cans) are the nut of choice around here. This flavorful nut grows on beautiful big trees and makes its way into Texas cuisine from appetizers and entrees to delicious desserts. Around the holidays we enjoy digging into big bowls of them, seasoned and toasted.

Texas is also famed for fabulous fruits. You can get your cantaloupe from Pecos in West Texas, watermelon from Luling, strawberries from Poteet, oranges from Mission, Ruby Red grapefruits from the Rio Grand Valley, and juicy blueberries from East Texas. Now if you can't come up with a great fruit salad with that combo, check out the recipe section in this book. I even toss in some pecan halves.

Being entertained in a typical Texas home may bring you in contact with some unfamiliar appetizers. You may be offered a hot spicy cheese dip made with Ro-Tel tomatoes and Velveeta cheese mixed and heated, or Texas caviar, which has nothing to do with fish eggs. It's those lucky black-eyed peas seasoned with onion and garlic. Armadillo eggs have nothing to do with armadillos, either, as they are fried peppers stuffed with cheese. If you are served some innocent-looking green jelly with cream cheese on crackers, beware; it's made from jalapeños and is habit forming. If you reach for the calf fries, know that you are fixin' to ingest what Coloradians euphemistically call Rocky Mountain Oysters and what Wyomingites not so delicately refer to as bull's balls— you heard me.

Because six flags have flown over Texas (Spanish, French, Mexican, Republic of Texas, Confederate, and Old Glory), you will find a wide variety of cuisine: from the Southern traditions and soul food with grits, greens, fried chicken, and baby-back ribs to the East Texas inspired French traditions of Creole and Cajun gumbos, jumbalayas, and etoufees. Around Fredericksburg in the heart of the Hill Country, rich German fare is celebrated year round, and these communities really roll out the carpet for Octoberfest. The Greek, Czech, and Danish traditions are also represented. Kolaches are a pastry delicacy you will find at many fairs, and the Polish communities have made sauerkraut popular around the state. Asian cultures are honored in Chinese, Japanese, Thai, and Vietnamese restaurants. Local fairs are great places to try all of the wonderful tastes from around the world, right here in Texas.

Baffling Booze News

≳ ★ ≲

I was in Piggly Wiggly the other day when a man in Bermuda shorts and shades queried the manager as to the whereabouts of the "wine aisle"; well, now he was definitely not from around here. The manager answered in a whisper so as not to offend other shoppers, "Sir, this is a dry county." The tourist scratched his head and asked, "Then where will I find a liquor store?" "Not in this county, Sir," was the polite reply.

There are still quite a few dry counties in Texas. Some of them do seem to be vying for the title of "Wettest Dry County." If you order a glass of wine with your meal in a lovely restaurant, you may be asked if you are a "member." Don't panic, you are not in Utah, and the "membership fee" will probably be minimal. Nowadays most establishments just use your drivers license number to find your membership number stored on the computer.

Dry counties are usually surrounded by profitable liquor stores just beyond their borders. This means that folks have to drive quite a ways and then really stock up once they get there—makes all kinds of nice folks feel like bootleggers. Check your Texas laws, you might just be one yourself. To get real technical the wet/dry issue can be voted on at the precinct level. Dallas County has places wet on one side of the street and dry on the other—go figure, only in Texas.

You may be surprised to know that Texas is producing some very fine wines these days. Winemaking began in the Spanish missions over three hundred years ago, and today we are the fifth largest wine-producing state in the nation. Our climate is quite similar to wine regions in Europe, and immigrants brought expertise in the cultivation and production of wine when they settled here.

Grapevine was settled in 1844 in wild mustang grape country. This grape is strong and actually disease-resistant—so much so that it was this rootstock that helped to save the great French vineyards from destruction when they were struck by disease in the late nineteenth century. The oldest winery in Texas is the Val Verde Winery near Del Rio on the Mexico border. The owner, Frank Qualia, was an Italian immigrant who managed to survive the Prohibition years by selling his grapes for table use. Val Verde has been honored by the Texas Grape Growers Association.

Today there are more than twenty producing wineries, and many are award winners. This can be an invigorating way to spend a Saturday, touring one of the wineries and learning about the process from the owners and their staff. The Messina Hof winery offers outdoor festivals with musical entertainment on their beautiful grounds located between College Station and Madisonville. Another I have visited is in Cedar Park, the Hill Country Cellars, where the staff was very helpful and informative. You can also learn about tannins, oak and fruity flavors, and be qualified to refer to a wine as "provocative" or "insolent" like a wine pro. Lubbock offers both Cap Rock and Llano Estacado wineries, and for an inexpensive white table wine, Ste. Genevieve can't be beat. Texans enjoy introducing out-of-state guests to the pleasures of great Texas wines.

Texas also brews some wonderful beers, with the Lone Star Buckhorn Saloon in San Antonio a must see. Visit the brewery and then tour the museum's collection of outstanding horns, animal horns that is. The oldest independent brewery in Texas is the Spoetzl Brewery that produces the ever-popular Shiner.

The Brew Kettle Museum in Fort Worth actually traces the history of beer making all the way back to ancient times. The story of the Miller Brewing Company is featured with memorabilia, souvenirs to purchase, and if you are over twenty-one, you can even sample the brews.

Microbreweries and brewpubs have become quite popular in recent years. The Metroplex and Austin area abound with brewed-on-the-premises pubs and bars that spotlight beers from around the world. The Texas Beer Festival Association holds events around the state to encourage the support of Texas beers. Be sure to stop in at the Fredericksburg Brewing Company when you are in that burg for great beer and some good eats.

Someone's in the Kitchen with Me

Writing a cooking column for the *Dublin Citizen* has been a real pleasure as I have been invited into the kitchens of some wonderful cooks and watched them do their magic. My great-grandmother and grandmother were both wonderful cooks, and my mom taught me to love cooking for friends and family. I also love to find great Texas cookbooks. Some places you might want to look for some interesting additions to your collection: church groups, local organizations, family reunions, and special Texas brand companies. Have fun with recipes and use them as a springboard for your own unique cookin'. To help you feel at home in Texas, I am including some recipes that cover a few of the basics, and I hope you will share them with those you love.

Armadillo Eggs

No, you are not eating armadillo eggs for real, but as I warned you, Texans like to mess with you.

1   pound Monterey Jack or cheddar cheese, grated and divided
1   pound spicy pork sausage
20 small to medium canned jalapeño peppers
1½ cups buttermilk biscuit mix
1   package Shake 'n Bake mix coating
2   eggs, beaten

Clean and seed peppers and stuff with half the cheese and close tightly. Mix remaining cheese and sausage, adding the dry biscuit mix a little at a time to make a stiff dough. Divide off a bit of dough and pat flat to about 1/2 inch thick. Put one stuffed pepper in the middle of each and cover the pepper totally, sealing the edges. Then shape the covered pepper carefully in your hands to form an egg shape. Dip in beaten egg and roll in the Shake 'n Bake mix. Place on a cookie sheet and bake at 300 degrees for 25-30 minutes until golden brown.

Toasted Spicy Pecans

¼ cup vegetable oil
1 egg white
1 tablespoon Worcestershire sauce
5-6 shots of Tabasco sauce
¼ teaspoon black pepper
¼ teaspoon cayenne pepper
½ teaspoon salt
1 teaspoon paprika
2 cups pecans

Combine ingredients in large bowl and mix well. Spread in single layer on large cookie sheet. Let stand for 10 minutes. Bake at 300 degrees for 25-30 minutes, stirring every 10 minutes. Move onto waxed paper and cool completely. Store in zip-lock baggies in refrigerator. (There won't be any to store because they'll be eaten as fast as you can make them.)

The Classic Pecan Pie

The best pecan pies I ever made were made from the recipe on the back label of Karo Syrup. I like to use the dark corn syrup, but the light works well, too. Please try this recipe, and it may become a holiday tradition at your home, too.

3   eggs, slightly beaten
1   cup sugar
1   cup Karo light or dark corn syrup
2   tablespoons margarine or butter, melted
1   teaspoon vanilla
1¼ cups pecans
1   (9-inch) unbaked or frozen deep-dish piecrust

Preheat oven to 350 degrees. In a large bowl stir the first five ingredients until well blended. Stir in pecans. Pour into piecrust. Bake 50-55 minutes or until knife inserted halfway between center and edge comes out clean. Cool on wire rack.

Banana Pudding

For some reason, any tough cowboy or oil rig rough-neck can be purring like a kitty when fed a bowl of banana pudding. Exactly why, I'm not sure. They just say, "My momma used to make it like that." This is my momma's recipe.

6   eggs, beaten
1   cup sugar
2   tablespoons all-purpose flour

1½ cups milk (a bit more if needed)
1 tablespoon vanilla
1 box vanilla wafers
2 sliced bananas

Mix sugar, flour, and milk in a saucepan and set over low heat. Gradually add eggs, stirring constantly. Cook, stirring often, over low heat until thickened. Remove from heat and add the vanilla. Line serving dish with vanilla wafers and half of the sliced bananas, then half of pudding and layer again with wafers, bananas, and top with remaining pudding. Refrigerate until ready to serve—at least 2-3 hours.

Pecan Pralines

When you finish a good Tex-Mex meal, the real topper is a cup of rich hot coffee and a pecan praline. These are as good as it gets!

1½ cups sugar
½ cup brown sugar
¾ cup evaporated milk
3 tablespoons light corn syrup
2 cups pecan halves
¼ teaspoon vanilla

Mix the sugars, milk, and syrup in a saucepan and bring to a boil, stirring constantly. Add the pecans and continue cooking until the mixture can be dropped (just a drop) into ice water and forms a soft ball. Then remove it from the heat, add the vanilla and margarine, and stir until the praline mixture turns dull. Drop spoonfuls onto wax paper to desired size.

Texas Caviar

2   cans black-eyed peas, rinsed and drained
1   finely chopped green bell pepper
1   finely chopped 1015 Texas onion
2   finely chopped and seeded jalapeños
1   small jar chopped pimientos
1   package Italian dressing mix
1   tablespoon wine vinegar
½   teaspoon garlic powder
Hot sauce to taste (Tabasco or Louisiana Hot)

Combine all ingredients and refrigerate overnight. Serve with round tortilla chips or as a relish with meats.

Layered Tex-Mex Dip

There are many variations of this party dip, but I found this one in the delightful *Diamonds in the Desert* cookbook that was compiled by the Ozona Women's League of Ozona, Texas. It was submitted by Becky Childress and Nancy Vannoy.

3   medium ripe avocados
2   tablespoons lemon juice
½   teaspoon salt
¼   teaspoon pepper
1   cup sour cream
½   cup mayonnaise or salad dressing

1   package taco seasoning mix
2   cans bean dip
1   cup chopped green onions with tops
2   3½-ounce cans chopped ripe olives
2   cups chopped tomatoes
8   ounces cheddar cheese, grated

Peel, pit, and mash the avocados with the lemon juice, salt, and pepper. Combine the sour cream, mayonnaise, and taco seasoning mix. Spread the bean dip in a large shallow platter or in a 9x13 inch casserole dish. Top with avocado mixture. Layer with taco seasoned mixture. Sprinkle top with the onions, tomatoes, and olives. Cover with the cheese. Serve chilled or at room temperature with round tortilla chips. (It's pretty in a clear glass dish to show off the layers.)

Killer Biscuits (AKA - Angel Flake)

This wonderful recipe comes from Texas chefette Carol Gibson, who with partner, Stormy Armstrong, is famous around these parts for great catering and a lovely restaurant—Cafe Trifles. Carol says this recipe was given to her by a woman who is serving time in prison for killing her husband. "These are the best biscuits ever, and the recipe makes about fifty—enough to feed the whole cell-block," she says.

Dissolve one package of yeast in five tablespoons of warm water.

Sift together:
5   cups flour

5   teaspoons baking powder
½   teaspoon soda
1½   teaspoons salt
3   tablespoons sugar

Cut 1 cup shortening into dry mixture until you reach a coarse crumb texture. Bring 2 cups buttermilk to room temperature and add to yeast mixture.

Mix all together; turn out on lightly floured board and pat out to one inch thick; cut biscuits. Bake at 350 degrees until golden brown or place on cookie sheet and freeze. When frozen store in plastic bags in freezer. Makes 50 biscuits.

Stormy's Mushroom Turnovers

When Carol and Stormy are not catering a wedding reception, political rally, social organization meeting, company party, or cooking and serving up beautiful lunches at Cafe Trifles, they are hosting a very informative and totally hilarious radio program called "Bakerstreet" on KSTV out of Stephenville. Stormy graciously offers this fancy appetizer to add some class to my Texas recipe collection. Stormy and Carol have a cookbook coming out soon. I know it will be a winner, coming from those two fireballs.

3   (3-ounce) packages of cream cheese
½   cup margarine
1½   cups flour
½   cup minced mushrooms
1   small onion, chopped finely

½   teaspoon salt

2   tablespoons flour

¼   cup sour cream

1   egg, beaten

Mix first three ingredients. Form a ball. Wrap in plastic wrap and chill. After dough has chilled several hours, sauté onions and mushrooms in 3 tablespoons margarine. Stir in remaining ingredients (except egg). Set aside.

Roll out dough about 1/8 inch thick. Cut in circles with round cookie cutter. Place 1/2 teaspoon of mushroom mixture in center. Seal edges with fork. Brush with egg and bake at 350 degrees for 12-15 minutes. May be stored unbaked in refrigerator for several days or frozen. May be baked straight from the freezer. Makes 55 turnovers and should be served warm or on a hot tray.

Green Chili Corn Bread

Here is another great idea from *Diamonds in the Desert* cookbook. Carmen Sutton submitted this variation on plain ol' corn bread.

1½   cups yellow cornmeal

½   cup flour

1   teaspoon salt

3   teaspoons baking powder

2   tablespoons sugar

1   egg

2   tablespoons oil

2   4-ounce cans green chilies, chopped

1   17-ounce can cream style corn
¾   cup grated sharp cheese

Place oiled 9x11 inch pan in 425 degree oven while preparing recipe. Blend dry ingredients well. Add milk and stir. Add egg and stir. Add remaining ingredients and mix well. Sprinkle hot oiled pan with cornmeal before pouring mixture into it. Bake about 50 minutes. Cut into squares.

King Ranch Chicken Casserole

As far as anybody can figure, the relationship between this recipe and the massive King Ranch is zip, zero, and zilch. First of all the King Ranch wasn't the Chicken Ranch, which passed into posterity as the Broadway musical *The Best Little . . .* you know, *in Texas*. No, the King Ranch was established by Captain Richard King back in 1853, is a cattle ranch and covers some 800,000 acres. But they give out the recipe on cute cards with a bonus recipe—a beef version.

1   can cream of chicken soup
1   can cream of mushroom soup
2   cups of chicken broth
1   can Ro-Tel tomatoes with green chilies
12 tortillas, cut in pieces
1   3-4 pound chicken, cooked and cut into bite-sized pieces
1   large onion, chopped
2   cups grated American cheese

Combine the soups, chicken broth, and tomatoes. Oil a 3-quart casserole. Cover bottom of dish with half of tortilla pieces, half of chicken, half of onion, and half of cheese. Pour half of soup mixture over. Repeat tortillas, chicken, and onion, then rest of soup mixture and top with remaining cheese. Bake at 350 degrees for 50 to 60 minutes. Even better the next day or after freezing.

Chicken-Fried Steak with Cream Gravy

How we figure this favorite Texas dish got started will crack you up. On long trail drives sometimes those ol' boys got plum sick of beef every night and started dreaming of some good ol' fried chicken. So one enterprising cookie got the idea to fry up some beef with a batter coating, and nowadays restaurants are serving up "Chicken-Fried Chicken Steaks" so there's no confusion. Right!

2   pounds round steak
1   cup flour
1   teaspoon salt
1   teaspoon pepper
2   eggs, beaten
¼   cup milk or buttermilk
Garlic salt to taste

Cut the steak into serving size pieces. Tenderize with a meat mallet or with the edge of a plate. (Beat it good!) Season and beat some more. Flour steaks (beat some more) and dip in combined milk/egg mixture, then back in the flour. Let set while you heat up deep, hot grease, then fry until golden brown. Drain on paper towels.

Cream Gravy

4   tablespoons pan drippings
3 to 4 tablespoons flour
2 to 3 cups milk
Salt and pepper to taste

Pour off all but 4 tablespoons of grease and blend in flour with whisk or fork. Slowly stir in milk and continue cooking and stirring and scraping all the stuck stuff off the bottom ('cause it tastes good) until thickened. Taste and season.

Not Jumbo's Gumbo

My friend Bobby Williams taught me about Texas gumbo. He says, "The Cajuns think they own gumbo, but they do and they don't. In Concho County where I was raised, gumbo was any kind of soup thickened with unripe okra." His mom, Maggie, taught him to cook. She told me once that she taught all her kids, boys and girls, to cook, "so they would be self-reliant." Bobby's pretty redheaded wife, Hazel, cooks right along with him. They move around the kitchen as if choreographed. "She chased me 'til I caught her," he says. Hazel says, "It was love at first sight." Lots of love in that kitchen.

Bobby's gumbo includes canned tomatoes, "smashed," with onion, bell pepper, shrimp, chicken (cooked and boned), oysters, and boudain sausage, if available. Bobby lets the ingredients do the flavoring and the okra do the thickening.

Texas gumbo cooks will argue till the cows come home about the roux (that's the mix of shortening and flour that starts most gumbos). Should it be cooked until it's golden, golden brown, brown, rich brown, or mahogany? Experiment and taste what other cooks do. You'll find what you like. Or you can have some truly great gumbo at The Boudain Hut in Port Arthur and hear a singer, Mary Arnold, who sounds a lot like Patsy Cline.

Easy-Basic Gumbo

1   cup shortening (or half shortening and half margarine)
1   cup flour
2   onions, chopped
1   bell pepper, chopped
2   stalks celery, chopped
2   cloves garlic, chopped
2   cans Cajun style stewed tomatoes
2   cans chicken broth
1   small can tomato sauce
1   quart okra—fresh or frozen (chopped or whole)
1   teaspoon salt
1   teaspoon pepper
Cayenne pepper to taste
Louisiana hot sauce to taste
1   2-3 pound chicken (cooked and deboned)
1   pound shrimp (shelled/deveined)
½   pound crab meat
½   pound sausage
½   pound oysters
Filé powder

Make the roux by stirring flour with wooden spoon into heated shortening in large iron pan and stirring (don't take phone calls or answer the door). Continue cooking roux until it reaches the color of peanut butter. If it burns, throw it out and start over. When roux is a deep golden color add the chopped veggies and continue to cook until they are translucent. Slowly add chicken broth, stirring, add tomatoes, stirring, add tomato sauce, add okra, chicken meat, and sausage. Cook for 30 minutes, stirring occasionally and checking for thickness (add liquid if needed). Add shrimp, crabmeat, and oysters and cook 7 minutes. Taste and season with salt, peppers, and hot sauce. Serve in bowls with "island" of rice on side or in center of bowl. Filé powder can be added just before serving or passed at the table.

Velveeta Ro-Tel Chicken Casserole

The ultimate family casserole that includes all of the Texas home-cook's emergency on-hand ingredients. Laugh if you must, but your family will love it.

5   cups cooked cubed chicken
1   can cream of mushroom soup
1   can cream of chicken soup
1   can Ro-Tel tomatoes with chilies
2   cups cubed Velveeta cheese
1   roll Ritz crackers, crumbled

Mix soups and tomatoes. Layer in casserole—chicken, cheese, soup mixture. Repeat twice. Top with crackers, drizzle with melted margarine, and bake for 45 minutes. Trust me!

Texas Chili

This recipe comes from the wonderful *Austin Heritage Cook Book* produced by the Heritage Society of Austin with recipes submitted by Society members, their relatives, and friends. I've had my copy for many years and it is a treasure. This is a very traditional version offered by Mrs. J. Larry Hall (Jane). Remember, everyone has a little different take on this Texas favorite.

3	lbs. chuck, cut into cubes
2	tablespoons oil
2	cloves garlic, chopped
2	teaspoons cumin
4-6	tablespoons chili powder
3	tablespoons flour
1	tablespoon oregano
2	cans condensed beef broth, divided
1	teaspoon salt
¼	teaspoon pepper

Brown cubes of chuck in oil in a heavy pan over medium heat. Lower heat and add garlic, cumin, chili powder, and flour. Stir until meat is coated. Add oregano, 1½ cans beef broth, and salt and pepper. Simmer partially covered 1 hour and 30 minutes, stirring occasionally. Add remaining beef broth and cook 30 minutes longer. Cover and refrigerate overnight to enhance the flavors.

Mrs. Hall added, "If desired you may add cooked beans to the chili, but we like to use this as a topping for cheese enchiladas."

Gazpacho

This is a refreshing cold soup that is like having liquid salad. There are many versions—this is mine.

2	tomatoes, chopped
2	green bell peppers, chopped
1	cup celery, chopped
1	large onion, chopped
1	avocado, chopped
1	large can or jar of V-8
1	cucumber, chopped
½	cup parsley, chopped
½	cup cilantro, chopped
2	tablespoons wine vinegar
1	tablespoon Worcestershire sauce

Tabasco or Louisiana Hot Sauce to taste
Salt and pepper to taste
Sour cream

Puree half of all vegetables in batches in blender. Combine puree and V-8 with remaining chopped veggies, leaving a few behind for garnish. Refrigerate several hours, preferably overnight. Serve in bowls topped with a dollop of sour cream and a sprinkling of chopped veggies, chopped parsley, and cilantro.

Weekend Breakfast Burritos

When I have guests for brunch, I often whip up these easy-to-fix easy-to-eat burritos. Add the ingredients you prefer or set bowls of fixings on the table and let family and friends choose what they like. It's a great way to feed a bunch of hungry folks fast!

8-12 eggs
1   tablespoon margarine/butter
8-12 (8-inch) flour tortillas
2   cups cheddar cheese/jack or combination
½   can pinto beans, drained
8   slices crispy fried bacon, crumbled
Salsa

Scramble eggs in margarine, adding 1 tablespoon salsa. Toss in beans and bacon. Spoon egg mixture evenly onto each tortilla, topping with 1 table-spoon cheese. Roll each tightly and place seam down in ungreased 13x9 inch backing dish, sprinkling cheese over top. Bake at 400 degrees until cheese melts. Serve with sour cream and more salsa. Fruit makes a nice side dish.

Taco Salad

Being born and bred in Texas, I grew up thinking "salad" meant shredded iceberg lettuce with a thin slice of tomato and a choice of French, Italian, or Thousand Island dressing, all mayonnaise based. Other salads included potato and macaroni, and that was about it. Nowadays on a hot Texas day we can serve our families a complete meal that is filling, tasty, and nutritious. Let them eat salad!

1	pound ground beef
1	package taco seasoning
1	tomato, chopped
1	onion, chopped
½	head iceberg lettuce, shredded
1	package shredded combination Mexican cheeses

Your favorite or homemade salsa

Sour cream

Brown ground beef and add taco seasoning. Place lettuce in bowls and top with meat, cheese, onion, tomato and cheeses. Top with dollop of sour cream and salsa. If you want to serve in those fancy tortilla bowls like in a restaurant, spray bottom of a metal bowl with nonstick spray, lightly spray large tortillas, and drape over inverted bowl. Bake in 400 degree oven for several minutes until golden and let cool. Cool, huh?

Texas Fruit Salad

Your local supermarket will probably feature Texas fruits at the height of their season. Grab up a passel and have some fun wowing your visitors with the beautiful bounty.

1	quart Pecos cantaloupe cut in 1-inch chunks
1	quart Luling watermelon cut in 1-inch chunks

4   Mission oranges, peeled and cut into segments
1   quart sliced peaches from Comanche County
2   Ruby Red grapefruit, cut into segments
1   pint Poteet strawberries
1   pint blueberries from East Texas
1   cup Texas pecan halves
1   bottle poppy seed dressing

Combine all ingredients and add any other fruits (apples, bananas, kiwi) to your liking in a very large bowl and dress with poppy seed dressing. Refrigerate until served.

Guacamole (Joe T. Garcias)

2   avocados, mashed
1   tomato, chopped
¼   onion, chopped
⅓   cup cilantro, chopped
1   serrano pepper, finely chopped
Juice of ½ lemon
Salt to taste

Mix all ingredients and serve with tortilla chips, on lettuce as salad, or as an addition to fajitas.

Pico de Gallo

2   large ripe tomatoes, chopped
1   large onion, chopped
½   cup cilantro leaves, chopped

Juice of 1 lime
1½ teaspoons olive oil
Salt, pepper, and hot sauce to taste

Combine all ingredients and chill. Serve with chips. Can accompany any meal, but is especially good with fish.

Fried Chicken Like My Grandma's

My mom's mom, Adele, was a fabulous Texas cook who never felt that dinner was ready until the table was so totally covered with steaming bowls and platters that there was barely room for place settings. She almost always served a couple of meat dishes and expected us to "take some from each now." Usually she would serve a pot roast (falling off the bone) or a clove-studded ham or maybe some ribs. But there was always fried chicken.

She taught us how just by letting us watch her in the kitchen. I always thought she soaked the chicken in buttermilk just because she personally liked it. Sooo, when I tried it on my own I used plain milk instead, and well, it was not quite as good. From then on I figured that Grandma really did know best.

Grandma gave me a full set of her favorite recipes when I got married and wrote little personal notes to highlight each. On the fried chicken page she added, "Your man will be home for dinner early for this!"

1   fryer, cut in serving pieces
1   quart buttermilk
3   cups flour
3   teaspoons seasoned salt
½   teaspoon garlic powder

½ teaspoon onion powder
1 teaspoon black pepper
Vegetable oil to fill a large iron skillet almost
    half full

Put the chicken pieces in large heavy-duty zip-pered bags, cover with buttermilk, and zip tightly closed. Refrigerate overnight—6-8 hours. When ready to cook, mix flour with spices—more if you like and use your imagination! Put a cup of flour in a large baggie with three chicken pieces and shake. Repeat until all are coated. Heat oil to frying tem-perature, around 350 degrees, and put in just enough pieces to fit comfortably. Fry until golden brown.

Adele's Country Baked Ham

Grandma served hams and turkeys like the rest of us might serve meat loaf—no holiday required. She did believe that Thanksgiving required a turkey and for Easter you needed a ham, but Christmas you needed both. She generally started with a canned ham and always turned it into a thing of beauty. Her note on this one read, "Good for Sunday dinner after church, espe-cially if the preacher is coming."

1 4-6 pound cooked ham
Jar of cloves
1 box brown sugar
1 can sliced pineapple
Jar of maraschino cherries

Place ham in foil-lined pan and score top into dia-monds. Place one clove in middle of each diamond.

Cover with half of brown sugar and bake for 1½ hours at 350 degrees. Pull it out, pat on rest of brown sugar, place pineapple slices on top to cover, and place cherries in middle of each and in between. Continue baking for 30 minutes, glazing with juices. Let rest for 15 minutes before carving.

Good Luck Black-Eyed Peas

On New Year's Day Texans join Southerners in partaking of the revered little peas that promise good luck for the coming year. We like ours spicy and actually eat them year round, but the New Year's tradition is a must. I was hosting a midnight dinner party one such holiday while I was living in Colorado. I served the spread buffet style. As I was checking to see what dishes needed to be replenished, I noticed that the large pot of peas had not been touched. I had to explain that each guest's fortunes would be secure with the addition of a small portion of the peas. One gentleman said, "I thought it was clam sauce, and I'm allergic to seafood." Hope you will give them a try at least once a year.

    4   cans quality black-eyed peas or 6 cups
        fresh
    2   large onions, rough cut in 1/2-inch chunks
    3   (or more) garlic cloves, mashed and
        minced
    6   slices bacon, fried crisp
    Hot sauce to taste
    2 or 3 shots Worcestershire sauce

Tump all peas into slow cooker with other ingredients. Slow cook until house smells wonderful—at least two hours. Season with salt and pepper to taste. Add hot sauce and Worcestershire to taste. Serve in bowls (with corn bread on the side). Great with frozen whole okra added and cooked a couple of hours.

Yes We Do Eat Grits

Now, grits are not as bad as they sounds. If you have a fondness for Italian food, you have probably enjoyed polenta. (My friend Ann and I once went to three great restaurants in one day in Sacramento trying to find the best polenta, but I digress.) Grits perform in much the same fashion. We usually have them buttered with a big breakfast. There's no real mystery to the basic preparation; the directions are on the box. But you can jazz grits up by adding cheese, garlic, and lots of hot sauce. And Quaker makes a respectable instant that is ready in about a minute. Go ahead, try 'em.

Fried Catfish

2	cups yellow cornmeal
1	tablespoon paprika
1	tablespoon garlic salt
1	teaspoon black pepper
2-3	pounds catfish fillets
2	cups buttermilk/egg wash
2	cups shortening (Crisco)

Combine seasonings and cornmeal. Lightly salt fillets. Dip fillets in buttermilk/egg wash (you can combine or use one or the other) then roll in seasoned cornmeal. Heat shortening to good frying heat, and fry catfish until golden brown. Drain and serve hot with fat French fries.

Sunday Souper Supper

Since Sunday dinner at noon is usually a big meal, it follows that supper needs to be light. Frequently the meal is sandwiches composed of whatever the main-meal meat happens to be. Sometimes it's just some soup or a toasted sandwich. Here are some suppers that have been popular with my family for years.

Salmon (or Tuna) Croquettes

1	large can salmon (or 2 cans tuna)
½	cup chopped onion
½	cup chopped red bell pepper
1	small jalapeño, chopped
1	beaten egg

Fine bread crumbs
Vegetable oil

Strain the salmon until dry, saving the liquid, and put in bowl. Add onion, bell pepper, and jalapeño and mix. Add the egg and 1/4 cup crumbs, adding salmon liquid as needed. Mix and form into timbales or patties. Roll in bread crumbs and fry until golden brown. Serve with white sauce and green peas if desired.

Elegant Pecan Chicken

My mom gave me this recipe years ago and thinks she got it from the *Austin-American Statesman*. You can invite company over at the last minute and wow them with this easy but delicious main dish.

4   chicken breast halves, deboned
2   tablespoons honey
2   tablespoons Dijon mustard
½   cup finely crushed pecans

Pound breasts with meat mallet to flatten. Mix honey and mustard and slather on chicken. Press chicken pieces into plate of pecans to coat both sides. Place in a greased baking dish and bake at 350 degrees for 15 to 20 minutes. I serve it on a bed of brown rice with fruit salad. Now, invite someone to dinner!

Chunky Chicken Tortilla Soup

This is a great way to use up leftover chicken. Works well with turkey or beef, too. This is another recipe that you can use whatever you have on hand.

1   tablespoon oil
2   cups of cooked chicken, diced
3   cups chicken broth
4   corn tortillas cut in 1 x ½ inch strips
1   can Ro-Tel tomatoes
1   can Mexically corn
1   cup chopped onion
2   cloves garlic, minced

1   medium potato, peeled and chopped
3   tablespoons chopped fresh cilantro
½   teaspoon cumin
½   teaspoon dried oregano
½   teaspoon chili powder
¼   teaspoon ground red pepper

Sauté onion and garlic in oil in Dutch oven just until fragrant. Add potato, broth, and spices and bring to a boil. Reduce heat to low and simmer 10 minutes until potatoes are tender. Arrange tortilla strips in a single layer on ungreased cookie sheet and spray tortillas with nonstick cooking spray. Bake at 375 degrees for about 10 minutes until crisp. Cool on paper towels. Blend half of potato mixture in blender and return to pan. Stir in all other ingredients and cook over medium heat for 5-10 minutes. Place several strips in bottom of serving bowls and ladle in soup. Garnish with a dollop of sour cream and a couple of tortilla strips.

Top-Side Peach Cobbler

I have made this cobbler for years, but I had to go to the Betty Crocker web site (BettyCrocker@mail.genmills .com) to get the proper measurements for you. You can request any recipe or just tell them what you have on hand, and they'll come up with one for you.

1   cup Bisquick
¼   cup milk
1   tablespoon sugar
1   tablespoon butter, melted and cooled
     slightly

1   can (29 ounces) sliced peaches, drained
½   cup sugar
½   teaspoon cinnamon
½   teaspoon nutmeg
1   tablespoon butter

Heat oven to 450 degrees. Generously grease square cake pan (8" or 9"). Mix Bisquick, milk, 1 tablespoon sugar, and the melted butter with fork to a soft dough. Pat dough into prepared pan; arrange peaches on top. Mix 1/2 cup sugar, cinnamon, and nutmeg; sprinkle evenly over peaches. Dot with 1 tablespoon butter. Bake about 30 minutes. Cut into squares. Serve warm and, if desired, with light cream. Makes 8 servings. (I say serve with ice cream!)

Dixie's Delicious "Dump" Cake

My mother used this yummy little cake to get us kids to do just about anything she wanted us to. "Get to cleaning your rooms, I'm thinking about making a dump cake tonight." We'd be running around like chickens with our heads cut off getting to the cleaning. Try it on your kids.

1   can crushed pineapple, undrained
1   can cherry pie filling
1   package yellow cake mix
½   cup butter or margarine

Butter a cake pan and dump (or tump) in the pineapple and the cherry pie filling. Sprinkle on the cake mix and dot with butter. Bake at 350 degrees for 50-60 minutes or until browned.

Sweet Sorrow

⋛ ★ ⋚

Parting is such. I hope I've given you a good start on your Texas experience. It's been a pleasure to be your guide. I'd like to leave you with another of my Gran's stories. Just pull up close, like we did when we were kids, and watch her rock and listen to her story.

"Now your great-granddaddy, Eli, was a Texas Ranger, and that was the most honorable thing a man could be in those days. After defending women and children from varmints all over South Texas, he did eventually return to our place and helped me with the cattle. Times were hard, and he had heard that things were better in Roswell, New Mexico. Well, I sure didn't want to go to no Roswell, New Mexico! I sure hadn't planned on never leavin' my home—Texas.

"But things got worse, and I was afraid that we weren't gonna make it. I had the five children, your granddaddy among 'em, that I had to take care of. So finally he plumb wore me down. I agreed that we would drive the herd to New Mexico. We loaded up the covered wagons and packed what furniture we could and clothes and such, and off we took. I rode in the wagon that carried my cook stove, pots and pans, and cooking supplies.

"After a long day's drive, we would circle up, and the boys would take my rolled up 4x4 linoleum and lay it out on the ground. Then they'd haul out my iron cook stove, and I'd fire it up just as if I was at home in my kitchen. I'd make rice and beans mostly. We tired of rice and beans before we finally got to where we were headed. I just prayed and prayed that we would be all right. It was a hard trip, and all of my cattle didn't make it.

"But things quickly went from worse to worser than worst. The winter hit hard and bitter cold. It came up a blue norther. The cows started gettin' sick, and some of the hands just had to quit. They were real sorry, and we understood. I prayed and said, 'Lord, please let us be all right.' I looked Eli in the eyes one day, and there was tears—and him a Texas Ranger and all. Well, he told me to pack up, that we were movin' on that very day. We packed up quickly and pushed along what few scrawny animals was still alive, and off we went.

"Days and days went by, and then one day I saw it. I saw the sunlight break through the clouds. I saw the land I knew and loved. My prayers had been answered. We were headed home—to Texas!"

She was BORN AGAIN TEXAN! GOD BLESS TEXAS!

Sources and Recommended Readings

Books

Any book by Texas historians J. Frank Dobie or A. C. Greene should be required reading.

Any book by Larry McMurtry including the often-disparaged *Texasville*, which includes characters you will meet in Texas using other names.

Aggies Handbook: Stories, Stats and Stuff About Texas A&M Football. Sam Blair. Wichita Eagle & Beacon Pub., 1996.

Confessions of a Maddog: A Romp Through the High-Flying Texas Music and Literary Era of the Fifties to the Seventies. Jay Dunston Milner. University of North Texas Press, 1998.

Rose Mary Rumbley's Dallas Too. R. Rumbley. Eakin Publications, 1996; and *The Unauthorized History of Dallas, Texas*. Rose-Mary Rumbley. Eakin Publications, 1991.

Fixin' to Be Texan. Helen Bryant. Republic of Texas Press, 1999.

Home Spun: A Collection. Leon Hale. Winedale Publishing, 1997. Anything by Leon Hale.

The Love Song of J. Edgar Hoover. Kinky Friedman. Ballantine Books, 1996. Mad genius will make you blush and laugh out loud. Read a lot of Kinky if you dare.

More Texas Sayings Than You Can Shake a Stick At. Anne Dingus. Gulf Pub. Co., 1996.

"Read My Lips": Classic Texas Political Quotes. Kirk Dooley and Eben Price. Texas Tech University Press, 1995.

Texas Almanac. The Dallas Morning News. 1998, 1999.

Texas Towns from A to Z: Pronunciation Guide. Bill & Clare Bradfield. Three Forks Press, 1996.

Texas Wit & Wisdom. Wallace O. Chariton. Republic of Texas Press, 1992.

McMillan's Texas Garden Almanac. Mike Peters, Liz Pruitt, and Howard Garrett. Gulf Pub., 1999.

Texas Gardening: Answers from the Experts. Laura C. Martin. Taylor Pub., 1998.

Find the following books at used bookstores or from places that handle out of print books:

How to Be Texan. Michael Hicks. 1981, 1997

The Insider's Country Music Handbook. Joe Flint and Judy Nelson. 1993

Life's Too Short Not to Live it as a Texan. Peg Hein and Kathryn Lewis. 1991.

Longhorns Handbook: Stories, Stats and Stuff About Texas University Football. Wendell Barnhouse. 1996

Texas Music. Rick Coster. 1998; Well written, well researched, and easy to read.

Texas Politics in My Rearview Mirror. Waggoner Carr & Byron Varner. 1993.

Cookbooks

Austin Heritage Cookbook. Heritage Society of Austin. 1982, 1985.

The Authorized Texas Ranger Cookbook. Texas Rangers. 1994, 1995, 1996.

Diamonds in the Desert. Ozona Woman's League. 1987, 1989, 1994.

Tastes & Tales from Texas...With Love. Peg Hein and Kathryn Lewis. Hein & Associates, 1984.

Texas Country Reporter Cookbook. Bob Phillips, Inc. Phillips Production. Shearer Pub., 1990.

Top Texas Chefs Favorite Recipes. Ginnie Bivona and Sharry Buckner. Republic of Texas Press, 1999.

Magazines

D Magazine

Fort Worth, Texas

Frontier Times

Texas Co-op Power

Southern Living presents Texas Vacations

Texas 1996 Accommodation Guide

Texas Highways

Texas Monthly

Texas Monthly Biz

Texas Observer

Web Sites

www.about.com—Type Texas in the Search box

www.aol.com/webcenters—Search on Texas websites

www.bootscootin.com—Dancin' and such

www.happycampers.net—Camping sites. You know what I mean.

www.lsjunction.com—The ls stands for Lone Star. Good basic site.

www.pbrnow.com—Bull riding information

www.texasalmanac.com—Good source

www.texasmonthly.com—The best information on Texas on the web for my money. Rodeo, travel, shopping, and all such.

www.tpwd.state.tx.us—Hunting and fishing info and all about Texas parks

www.traveltex.com—Texas Department of Transportation official travel guide site

www.tsha.utexas.edu—Texas State Historical Association web site, includes a text-only online version of *The Handbook of Texas*

www.state.tx.us—Resources for citizens, visitors, businesses, and government

More humor and trivia from Republic of Texas Press

1-55622-648-9 • $15.95

1-55622-695-0 • $16.95

1-55622-653-5 • $17.95

1-55622-572-5 • $15.95

1-55622-526-1 • $12.95

1-55622-699-3 • $14.95

1-55622-257-2 • $12.95

1-55622-616-0 • $14.95

1-55622-683-7 • $16.95

Other books from

Republic of Texas Press

Mystery and History of the Menger Hotel

Mythic Texas: Essays on the State and its People

Our Texas Heritage

Pampered Cowboy

Phantoms of the Plains

Puncher Pie and Cowboy Lies

Rainy Days in Texas Funbook

Red River Women

Return of Assassin John Wilkes Booth

Southern Fried Spirits

Spindletop Unwound

Spirits of the Alamo

Spirits of San Antonio and South Texas

Tales of the Guadalupe Mountains

Texas Boys in Gray: Confederate War Letters

Texas Firehouse Cooks: Favorite Recipes

Texas Golf Guide (2nd Ed.)

Texas Heroes: A Dynasty of Courage

Texas Highway Humor

Texas Indian Myths and Legends

Texas Ranger Johnny Klevenhagen

Texas Ranger Tales

Texas Ranger Tales II

Texas Roadside Restaurants and Cafes

Texas Tales Your Teacher Never Told You

Texas Wit and Wisdom

That Cat Won't Flush

That Terrible Texas Weather

They Don't Have to Die

This Dog'll Really Hunt

Tom Dodge Talks About Texas

Top Texas Chefs: Favorite Recipes

Treasury of Texas Humor

Treasury of Texas Trivia

Treasury of Texas Trivia II

Ultimate Chili Cookbook

Uncle Bubba's Chicken Wing Fling

Unsolved Mysteries of the Old West

Unsolved Texas Mysteries

Volunteers in the Texas Revolution: The New Orleans Greys

When Darkness Falls